SPECTRUM®

Enrichment Math

Grade 7

Published by Spectrum®
an imprint of Carson-Dellosa Publishing LLC
Greensboro, NC

Spectrum® is an imprint of Carson-Dellosa Publishing.

Send all inquiries to:
Carson-Dellosa Publishing
P.O. Box 35665
Greensboro, NC 27425 USA

Printed in the USA   ISBN 978-0-7696-6337-1

02-090127811

Table of Contents Grade 7

Table of Contents, continued

NAME _____

Check What You Know

Whole Numbers

Read the problem carefully and solve. Show your work under each question.

Parville has a population of 8,124 children and 32,492 adults, for a total population of 40,616 people. Somerset has a total population of 358,412 people.

1. What is the difference between the number of adults and the number of children in Parville?

_____ people

2. What is the total population of Parville and Somerset?

_____ people

3. There is an average of 5 school textbooks per child in Parville. How many textbooks are there in total?

_____ textbooks

4. Parville surveys every 15th person in the town to see if there is support for a new library. How many people are surveyed?

_____ people

5. In Parville, every 4th child plays a sport. How many children play a sport?

_____ children

6. A new company moves into Parville, which brings 1,945 new residents. Assuming no one moves out, what is the total population of Parville now?

_____ people

Lesson 1.1 Adding and Subtracting through 6 Digits

Read the problem carefully and solve. Show your work under each question.

A national appliance store chain keeps track of the appliances it sells each year. Last year, the store sold 102,039 microwave ovens, 87,382 stoves, 45,392 refrigerators, 128,905 toaster ovens, and 72,682 blenders.

Helpful Hint

When two digits add up to more than 10, rename the digits and carry, if necessary. For example:

$$\begin{array}{r} \overset{1}{37} \\ + 65 \\ \hline 2 \end{array}$$

$7 + 5 = 12$

Rename 12 as "1 ten and 2 ones."

---

3. How many of the appliances sold were not microwave ovens?

_____ appliances sold were not microwave ovens

1. What is the total number of toaster ovens and blenders sold last year?

_____ toaster ovens and blenders

4. What is the total number of stoves and refrigerators the appliance store sold last year?

_____ stoves and refrigerators

2. How many more microwave ovens were sold than refrigerators?

_____ more microwaves were sold

5. How many more toaster ovens were sold than stoves?

_____ more toaster ovens were sold

Lesson 1.2 Multiplying through 4 Digits

Read the problem carefully and solve. Show your work under each question.

José manages the shipping department of a calculator manufacturing company. He ships calculators in 3 different types of boxes. A small box can hold 46 calculators, a medium box can hold 354 calculators, and a large box can hold 1,178 calculators.

Helpful Hint

When multiplying by a two-digit number (the bottom number), remember to put a zero in the ones place before you multiply the digit in the tens place of the bottom number by each digit in the top number.

1. If José ships 32 small boxes of calculators, how many calculators does he ship altogether?

_____ calculators

2. José ships 54 large boxes of calculators in one month. What is the total number of calculators shipped in that month?

_____ calculators

3. In another month, José ships 67 medium boxes of calculators. How many calculators does he ship in that month?

_____ calculators

4. A large school district orders 112 medium boxes of calculators. How many calculators will the school district receive?

_____ calculators

5. José receives an order for 125 large boxes of calculators to be shipped overseas. How many individual calculators will that order contain?

_____ calculators

Lesson 1.3 Dividing by 1 and 2 Digits

Read the problem carefully and solve. Show your work under each question.

A school district has 325 administrators, 2,462 teachers, and 43,920 students.

Helpful Hint

When dividing with whole numbers, you may find that the numbers do not divide evenly. The amount left is called a **remainder**.

1. The school superintendent decides to send every 4th teacher to a professional development workshop. How many teachers go to the workshop? What is the remainder?

_____ teachers

remainder _____

2. During an administrative meeting, the district administrators are divided into groups of 5. How many administrators are in each group?

_____ administrators

3. The school district has an event that includes every student in the district. The students take buses to this event and each bus holds 60 students. Assuming no students are absent, how many buses will be used to bus the students to the event?

_____ buses

4. During a professional development day for the teachers, the teachers are placed into groups of 40. Next, any remaining teachers will be added to a group. How many groups are there and how many remaining teachers need to be added to a group?

_____ group

_____ teachers need to be added to a group

5. If 30 students are in each class, at any given time during the school day, how many classes are in session in the district?

_____ classes

Check What You Learned

Whole Numbers

Read the problem carefully and solve. Show your work under each question.

Students from five different high schools collected cans of food to donate to a food bank. The table below shows the number of cans of food collected in one year at each school.

School	Kent	Midway	Rockville	Langley	Roxbury
# of Cans	9,058	28,250	36,424	100,264	94,550

1. What is the total number of cans collected at Midway and Roxbury schools?

   _____ cans

4. If Kent High School collects 3 times as many cans of food next year than listed in the table, how many cans will that total?

   _____ cans

2. What is the difference between the number of cans collected at Rockville High School and at Midway High School?

   _____ cans

5. The cans collected at Midway High School are put into boxes with 25 cans in each box. How many boxes are used?

   _____ boxes

3. What is the total number of cans collected at Langley and Roxbury high schools?

   _____ cans

6. Half of the cans collected at Kent High School are cans of vegetables. How many cans of vegetables are there altogether?

   _____ cans of vegetables

NAME _____

 # Check What You Know

Fractions

Read the problem carefully and solve. Show your work under each question.

Carlos is redesigning his dining room. The room measures $8\frac{1}{4}$ feet by $10\frac{1}{2}$ feet. He has several pieces of furniture that he plans to put in the room.

1. Carlos has two buffet tables. One table is $\frac{2}{3}$ yard wide and the other is $\frac{3}{4}$ yard wide. He wants to add the lengths of tables, so he finds the LCM for the denominators. What is the LCM of 3 and 4?

_____

2. Use the least common multiple to compare the widths of the buffet tables. What is the width of the wider table?

_____ _____ yard

3. If he places the two buffet tables side-by-side along the wall, what will be the total length of the tables? Show your answer in simplest form.

_____ yards

4. Carlos's dining table measures $6\frac{1}{2}$ feet in length, including a $1\frac{3}{4}$–foot leaf. If he removes the leaf, how long will the table be?

_____ feet

5. Carlos wants to know the area of the dining room. What is the total area in square feet?

_____ square feet

6. Carlos uses $2\frac{1}{2}$ cups of cleaning fluid to clean 6 chairs. If he uses the same amount of fluid on each chair, how much cleaning fluid is used on each chair?

_____ cup

Lesson 2.1 Finding the Greatest Common Factor

Read the problem carefully and solve. Show your work under each question.

Melinda owns a bread bakery. Each week, she bakes 32 loaves of multigrain, 48 loaves of white, 36 loaves of wheat, 24 loaves of pumpernickle, 18 loaves of rye, 12 loaves of raisin, and 27 loaves of oat bread.

Helpful Hint

To find the **greatest common factor** of two or more numbers, list all the factors for each number. Identify the factors that are the same (common) for each number. The largest of these factors is the greatest common factor.

1. Melinda wants to put equal batches of multigrain and white loaves of bread into bins. What is the greatest common factor of 32 and 48?

   _____

2. Melinda organizes the oat and wheat loaves of bread into equal batches to place in displays. What is the greatest common factor of 27 and 36?

   _____ and _____

3. Melinda organizes the loaves of pumpernickel and rye bread into equal batches to donate to a food bank. What is the greatest common factor of 24 and 18?

   _____

4. One week, Melinda puts the same number of multigrain and raisin loaves of bread into bags for delivery to restaurants. What is the greatest common factor of 32 and 12?

   _____

5. Another week, Melinda organizes the pumpernickel and white loaves of bread into equal groups to place in the store. What is the greatest common factor of 24 and 48?

   _____

Lesson 2.2 Reducing to Simplest Form

Read the problem carefully and solve. Show your work under each question.

The Fun Wheel at a carnival is divided into 60 equal sections. Five of the sections are green, 8 are blue, 9 are purple, 16 are orange, and 22 are yellow. Players choose a color and then spin the wheel. If the wheel stops on the color chosen, they win a prize based on that color.

Helpful Hint

To reduce a fraction to **simplest form**, divide both the numerator and denominator by their greatest common factor.

1. Lamont chooses yellow and there is a $\frac{22}{60}$ chance that the Fun Wheel will stop on yellow. Write $\frac{22}{60}$ in simplest form.

   _____

2. Anton chooses blue. There is an $\frac{8}{60}$ chance that the Fun Wheel will stop on blue. Write $\frac{8}{60}$ in simplest form.

   _____

3. Amira thinks that there is a $1\frac{9}{60}$ chance that the Fun Wheel will stop on purple. Explain why this is impossible.

   _____

   _____

   _____

4. Connor does not know what the likelihood is that the Fun Wheel will stop on orange. What is the likelihood that the wheel will stop on orange? Write your answer in simplest form.

   _____

5. Robert wants the Fun Wheel to stop on green. What is the probability that the wheel will stop on green? Write your answer in simplest form.

   _____

NAME _____

Lesson 2.3 Finding Common Denominators

Read the problem carefully and solve. Show your work under each question.

Mr. Johnston gives each student the same puzzle. He records how long it takes each student to complete the puzzle in fractions of an hour.

Marlene	Kareem	Bianca	Paul
$\frac{5}{6}$ hour	$\frac{2}{3}$ hour	$\frac{5}{12}$ hour	$\frac{5}{8}$ hour

Helpful Hint

To find a common denominator for two or more fractions, find the **least common multiple (LCM)** of the denominators. The least common multiple is the smallest multiple of both numbers.

3. Use the least common multiple to compare Marlene and Paul's times for completing the puzzle. Use >, <, or =.

_____

1. Mr. Johnston wants to compare the time it took Marlene and Bianca to complete the puzzle. Rename their times using the least common multiple for the denominator.

   Marlene _____

   Bianca _____

4. Mr. Johnston wants to compare all four students' times for completing the puzzle. What is the least common multiple of all the fractions in the table?

_____

2. Who completed the puzzle faster, Paul or Kareem?

_____

5. Which student completed the puzzle with the second fastest time?

_____

Lesson 2.4 Renaming Fractions and Mixed Numerals

Read the problem carefully and solve. Show your work under each question.

Natalie and Inez play a game. They each write three improper fractions and three mixed numerals on a piece of paper. They switch papers and rename the improper fractions as mixed numerals and the mixed numerals as improper fractions. They each get a point for every fraction and mixed numeral they rename correctly.

Helpful Hint

To rename a mixed numeral, multiply the whole number by the denominator and add the numerator to the product. This is the numerator of the renamed fraction. The denominator stays the same.

1. Inez has to rename $\frac{25}{7}$ as a mixed numeral. Write the correct mixed numeral.

   _____

2. Natalie rewrites $\frac{15}{4}$ as a mixed numeral. What is the mixed numeral she writes?

   _____

3. Inez has to rename the mixed numeral $4\frac{5}{8}$. Write the correct improper fraction on the line below.

   _____

4. Natalie writes $2\frac{2}{9}$ as an improper fraction. What fraction does she write?

   _____

5. Inez has to rename the mixed numeral $6\frac{3}{5}$. Write the correct improper fraction on the line below.

   _____

Lesson 2.5 Adding and Subtracting Fractions and Mixed Numerals

Read the problem carefully and solve. Show your work under each question.

Jared buys food for a party. He buys $\frac{5}{8}$ pound of roast beef, $\frac{6}{7}$ pound of ham, $\frac{3}{4}$ pound of chicken salad, $2\frac{2}{5}$ pounds of corned beef, $3\frac{2}{3}$ pounds of turkey, $1\frac{3}{4}$ pounds of havarti cheese, and $1\frac{1}{3}$ pounds of cheddar cheese.

Helpful Hint

To rename a mixed numeral, multiply the whole number by the denominator and add the numerator to the product. This is the numerator of the renamed fraction. The denominator stays the same.

1. How many pounds of roast beef and ham did Jared buy altogether?

_____ pounds

2. What is the difference between the amount of chicken salad Jared bought and the amount of roast beef he bought?

_____ pound

3. How many more pounds of turkey than corned beef did Jared buy?

_____ pounds

4. How many total pounds of ham and corned beef did Jared buy?

_____ pounds

5. How many more pounds of havarti cheese than cheddar cheese did Jared buy?

_____ pound

Lesson 2.6 Multiplying Fractions and Mixed Numerals

Read the problem carefully and solve. Show your work under each question.

Trey buys five different types of coffee beans. He buys $\frac{1}{2}$ pound of vanilla, $\frac{8}{9}$ pound of Columbian, $2\frac{1}{4}$ pounds of mild blend, $1\frac{1}{2}$ pounds of dark roast, and $3\frac{2}{3}$ pounds of hazelnut.

Helpful Hint

When multiplying mixed numerals, first rename the numbers as fractions. Then, reduce to simplest form, multiply the numerators and denominators, and simplify.

1. Trey ran out of mild blend too quickly. Next time, he will buy $1\frac{1}{2}$ times as much mild blend. How much mild blend will he buy next time?

   _____ pounds

2. The next time Trey buys coffee, he will multiply his order of dark roast by $2\frac{2}{3}$. How many pounds of dark roast will he order?

   _____ pounds

3. Next time, Trey will multiply his order of hazelnut coffee beans by 2. How many pounds of hazelnut coffee will he buy?

   _____ pounds

4. Trey sends $\frac{1}{2}$ the amount of vanilla coffee beans to his mother. How many pounds of vanilla coffee beans does he send?

   _____ pound

5. On his next visit to the store, Trey buys $\frac{1}{4}$ of the amount of Columbian coffee beans that he bought last time. How many pounds of Columbian coffee beans does he buy?

   _____ pound

Lesson 2.7 Reciprocals

Read the problem carefully and solve. Show your work under each question.

Mrs. Anderson wrote the following list numbers on the whiteboard. Then, she assigned each student one of the numbers.

$$\frac{15}{19} \quad 45 \quad 4\frac{5}{7} \quad \frac{4}{9} \quad 3\frac{2}{9}$$

Helpful Hint

Reciprocals are any two numbers with a product of 1. Rename a mixed numeral as a fraction to find the reciprocal.

1. Aaron was given $\frac{15}{19}$. What is its reciprocal?

   _____

2. Brooke has to write the reciprocal of 45. What does she write?

   _____

3. Jan was assigned the number $4\frac{5}{7}$. What is its reciprocal?

   _____

4. Camden writes the reciprocal of $\frac{4}{9}$. What does he write?

   _____

5. Hunter writes the reciprocal of $3\frac{2}{9}$. What does he write?

   _____

Lesson 2.8 Dividing Fractions and Mixed Numerals

Read the problem carefully and solve. Show your work under each question.

Emilio is cooking a roast turkey with stuffing for dinner. He uses a recipe given to him by his grandmother, but he plans to make some modifications to the recipe. The modifications he plans to make are explained in each question below.

Helpful Hint

To divide by a fraction, multiply by its reciprocal. If a problem has mixed numbers, rename them as fractions before you divide.

1. The recipe calls for 4 tablespoons of butter. Emilio wants to divide the amount of butter by $1\frac{3}{4}$. How much butter will he use?

   _____ tablespoons

2. The recipe calls for $2\frac{3}{4}$ teaspoons of salt. Emilio plans to divide this amount by $1\frac{1}{2}$. How much salt will he use?

   _____ teaspoons

3. The recipe calls for $6\frac{1}{2}$ cups of flour, but Emilio plans to divide this amount by $\frac{3}{4}$ because he is serving fewer people. How much flour will he use?

   _____ cups

4. The recipe calls for $1\frac{3}{4}$ cups of onion, but Emilio doesn't like onions. He plans to divide this amount by 2. How many cups of onion will he use?

   _____ cup

5. The recipe calls for $2\frac{1}{2}$ cups of celery, but one of Emilio's guests doesn't like celery, so he divides this amount by 2. How many cups of celery will he use?

   _____ cups

Check What You Learned

Fractions

Read the problem carefully and solve. Show your work under each question.

Demitri rents a new office space. The room measures $10\frac{3}{8}$ feet by $14\frac{3}{4}$ feet. He has several pieces of furniture that he plans to put in the office, as well as some decorative molding.

1. Demitri has two tables with different lengths. One is $\frac{7}{10}$ meter long and the other is $\frac{4}{5}$ meter long. He plans to put the tables together, so he finds the least common multiple of 5 and 10. What is the LCM?

   _____

2. Demitri compares the lengths of the tables using <, >, or =. Write a statement that compares the lengths of the tables.

   _____

3. Demitri puts the tables side-by-side to make one long table. What is the length of the tables together?

   _____ meters

4. Demitri buys a piece of molding that is $3\frac{5}{8}$ meters long. He cuts a piece $2\frac{1}{2}$ meters long to put on a wall. What is the length of the left over molding?

   _____ meters

5. Carlos wants to know the area of Demitri's office. What is the area of the office?

   _____ square feet

6. Demitri buys $12\frac{1}{3}$ yards of fabric to make 4 curtains. If he uses the same amount of fabric for each curtain, how much fabric does he use for each curtain?

   _____ yards

NAME _____

Check What You Know

Decimals

Read the problem carefully and solve. Show your work under each question.

Mischa works at an electronics store. She is in charge of ordering items and tracking sales.

1. If 15 TVs are sold for $324.99 each, what are the total sales for the TVs?

   _____

2. This year, the store sold $3\frac{3}{8}$ times more headphones than last year. Mischa needs to convert this number into a decimal for calculating inventory. What is $3\frac{3}{8}$ written as a decimal?

   _____

3. Mischa calculates that $556.50 in cameras was sold at the store. Using your answer for Question 1, what is the difference between the total sales for the TVs and the total sales for the cameras?

   _____

4. If $85.50 in earphones is sold and $590.88 in speakers is sold, what are the total sales for earphones and speakers?

   _____

5. A box of cameras weighs 16.055 pounds. If each camera weighs 1.235 pounds, how many cameras are in each box?

   _____ cameras

6. Mischa calculated that the store has 2.25 times more sales at night than during the day. If the sales during one day are $865.60, how much does Mischa expect the sales to be that night?

   _____

Lesson 3.1 Converting Decimals and Fractions

Read the problem carefully and solve. Show your work under each question.

Kenyon is organizing his CD collection into a CD tower. He is separating the CDs into different music categories.

Helpful Hint

To convert a decimal to a fraction, say the decimal out loud. To convert 0.75, say "seventy-five hundredths." This will help you write the fraction $\frac{75}{100}$, which simplifies to $\frac{3}{4}$.

1. While organizing his CDs, Kenyon realizes that $\frac{5}{40}$ of his CDs are from jazz artists. Write this fraction in decimal form.

   _____

2. Kenyon has $1\frac{3}{4}$ the amount of CDs that he had last year. What is $1\frac{3}{4}$ written as a decimal?

   _____

3. While organizing his CDs, Kenyon realizes that $\frac{57}{200}$ of his CDs are from alternative rock bands. Write this fraction in decimal form.

   _____

4. Kenyon calculated that 0.14 of his CDs are from hip-hop artists. Convert this decimal to a fraction.

   _____

5. The CD tower weighs 3.375 pounds. Convert 3.375 to a mixed numeral.

   _____

Lesson 3.2 Adding Decimals

Read the problem carefully and solve. Show your work under each question.

Elena is training for a race and using a pedometer to track the distances on runs. The decimals below show the number of kilometers she ran during 8 training runs.

Day 1	Day 4	Day 7	Day 10	Day 13	Day 17	Day 20	Day 23
5.38	7.935	2.45	10.56	8.425	15.048	17.5	6.2

Helpful Hint

When adding and subtracting decimals, keep the decimal points aligned. If the decimals have a different number of digits, add zeros as placeholders.

1. Elena ran the farthest during days 17 and 20. How many total kilometers did she run on these two days?

   _____ kilometers

2. How many total kilometers did Elena run on days 1 and 4?

   _____ kilometers

3. How many total kilometers did Elena run on the three shortest runs?

   _____ kilometers

4. How many total kilometers did Elena run on days 7, 10, and 13?

   _____ kilometers

5. Find the total number of kilometers Elena ran during her last three training runs.

   _____ kilometers

Lesson 3.3 Subtracting Decimals

Read the problem carefully and solve. Show your work under each question.

John has six containers with the volume written on the side of each container. The table below shows the number of ounces each container holds.

Container 1	Container 2	Container 3	Container 4	Container 5	Container 6
35.52 oz.	16.25 oz.	24.825 oz.	20.485 oz.	32.6 oz.	14.46 oz.

Helpful Hint

Before you subtract decimals, be sure to align the decimal points. Subtract the decimals as you would whole numbers. Align the decimal point in the answer with the decimal points above.

1. What is the difference between the number of ounces containers 1 and 2 hold?

    _____ ounces

2. How many more ounces can container 5 hold than container 6?

    _____ ounces

3. What is the difference between the number of ounces containers 3 and 2 hold?

    _____ ounces

4. What is the difference of the volumes of the largest container and the smallest container?

    _____ ounces

5. How many more ounces can container 1 hold than container 5?

    _____ ounces

Lesson 3.4 Multiplying Decimals

Read the problem carefully and solve. Show your work under each question.

Kyle is reading some of the nutrition labels for the food in his cabinet. He wants to determine the amount of the food he eats.

Helpful Hint

When multiplying decimals, count the number of decimal places in each factor. The sum of the decimal places tells you how many digits should be to the right of the decimal point in the product.

1. The cereal Kyle eats contains 8.1 ounces per serving. If he eats 1.75 servings, how many total ounces of cereal does he eat?

   _____ ounces

2. The beans Kyle eats contain 8.5 grams of protein per serving. If he eats 2.15 servings, how many total grams of protein does he eat?

   _____ grams

3. Kyle has 5 containers of almonds. Each container has 9.5 ounces of almonds. How many total ounces of almonds does he have?

   _____ ounces

4. One serving of salad dressing has 2.5 grams of fat. How many grams of fat are in 0.75 serving?

   _____ grams

5. If Kyle eats 1.7 servings of rice, and each serving contains 14.5 grams of carbohydrates, how many total grams of carbohydrates does Kyle eat?

   _____ grams

Lesson 3.5 Dividing Decimals by Whole Numbers

Read the problem carefully and solve. Show your work under each question.

Sara's mom takes her shopping to buy some clothes.

Helpful Hint

When dividing a decimal by a whole number, place the decimal point in the quotient directly above the decimal point in the dividend.

Example:
$$5)\overline{10.55} \quad 2.11$$

1. Sara spends $56.60 on 4 shirts that each cost the same amount. What is the price of each shirt?

   _____

2. Sara spends $65.98 for 2 pairs of shoes. If each pair costs the same, what does each pair of shoes cost?

   _____

3. Sara buys a package of 12 pairs of socks. If the package costs $23.76, what is the cost per pair of socks?

   _____

4. Sara buys 3 of the same type of dress, but in different colors. If she spends a total of $80.34, how much does each dress cost?

   _____

5. Sara wants to ship 2 pairs of her new pants to her cousin. She weighs the pants at the shipping store. The weight of both pairs of pants is 2.3568 pounds. How much does one pair weigh?

   _____ pounds

Lesson 3.6 Dividing Whole Numbers by Decimals

Read the problem carefully and solve. Show your work under each question.

Arianna works at a restaurant. She is separating large amounts of food into servings for cooking.

Helpful Hint

Multiply the divisor and the dividend by the same power of 10 to change the divisor to a whole number.

Example: $0.25\overline{)10.5}$ → $25\overline{)1050}$

Multiply by 100

3. Arianna is making patties from 21 pounds of ground beef. If each patty weighs 0.35 pound, how many patties will there be?

_____ beef patties

1. Arianna has 48 pounds of potatoes. Each serving of potatoes is 1.2 pounds. How many servings are in 48 pounds?

_____ servings

4. There are 51 pounds of salmon. If Arianna divides the salmon into 0.3-pound portions, how many portions will she have?

_____ portions

2. There are 12 pounds of shrimp. If Arianna divides the shrimp into 0.25-pound portions, how many portions will she have?

_____ portions

5. Arianna weighs a bag of salt that she will divide evenly into 6 smaller bags. If the bag weighs 6.8052 pounds, how much will each smaller bag weigh?

_____ pounds

Lesson 3.7 Dividing Decimals by Decimals

Read the problem carefully and solve. Show your work under each question.

Lee is a farmer who sells his produce to local grocery stores. Today, he has 22.5 pounds of broccoli, 8.4 pounds of lettuce, 6.8 pounds of green peppers, 1.8 pounds of basil, and 38.25 pounds of tomatoes.

Helpful Hint

To divide a decimal by a decimal, multiply the divisor and the dividend by the same power of 10 to change the divisor to a whole number.

1. Lee divides the broccoli into 0.75-pound portions. How many portions does he have?

_____ portions

2. Lettuce is sold in bags that weigh 0.2 pound each. How many bags of lettuce will be filled with Lee's lettuce?

_____ bags

3. Lee divides the green peppers into 0.4-pound portions. How many portions does he have?

_____ portions

4. Basil is divided into 0.06-pound packets. How many packets will be filled with Lee's basil?

_____ packets

5. The grocer gives Lee bags for packing his vegetables. The total weight of the bags is 9.2442 pounds. If each bag weighs 0.035 pound, how many bags are there? Give your answer as a decimal and also as the nearest whole number.

_____ about _____ bags

Check What You Learned

Decimals

Read the problem carefully and solve. Show your work under each question.

Anna works at her father's kitchen supply store. A set of pots and pans sells for $229.59. A set of glasses sells for $74.10. A frying pan sells for $38.98.

1. If Anna sells 12 sets of pots and pans, what are her total sales for pots and pans?

   _____

2. If a set of glasses contains 6 glasses, what is the sale price per glass?

   _____

3. Anna sells 5 frying pans. What is the difference between her total sales for the frying pans and 12 sets of glasses?

   _____

4. On one day, Anna sells one set of glasses and $459.18 in sets of pots and pans. What are her total sales for the day?

   _____

5. A box of frying pans from the supplier weighs 38.88 pounds. If each pan weighs 3.24 pounds, how many pans are in the box?

   _____

6. Anna sold 2.56 times more in the winter than in the summer. Write 2.56 as a fraction.

   _____

Check What You Know

Finding Percents

Read the problem carefully and solve. Show your work under each question.

Chrissie works at a fabric store. She orders fabric once a month.

1. Chrissie orders 25% of her fabric from the same vendor each month. Write 25% as a decimal.

_____

4. Write the following numbers in order from least to greatest.
0.35, 34%, $\frac{1}{3}$

_____

2. She orders $1\frac{3}{4}$ yards of blue fabric and 1.7 yards of red fabric. Compare $1\frac{3}{4}$ and 1.7 using <, >, or =.

_____

5. In January, $\frac{3}{25}$ of the fabric she ordered was textured. Write $\frac{3}{25}$ as a percent.

_____

3. Chrissie orders 30% more fabric in December. Write 30% as a fraction in simplest form.

_____

6. In March, Chrissie orders 40 yards of fabric. 15% of the order was for lining fabric. How many yards of lining fabric did Chrissie order?

_____ yards

Lesson 4.1 Understanding Percents

Read the problem carefully and solve. Show your work under each question.

Mrs. Adams gave a science test to her class last week. The following are test scores for five of her students:

78% 80% 65% 94% 88%

Helpful Hint

Any percent can be written as a fraction with a denominator of 100. Percents can also be written as decimals by removing the percent symbol and dividing the number by 100 (the decimal point moves 2 places to the left).

25% $\frac{25}{100}$ 0.25

1. Javier scored 78% on the test. Write this percent as a fraction in simplest form and as a decimal.

   _____ and _____

2. Carly scored 80% on the test. Write this percent as a fraction in simplest form and as a decimal.

   _____ and _____

3. Andrew received a 65% on the test. Write this percent as a fraction in simplest form and as a decimal.

   _____ and _____

4. Rebecca scored 94% on the test. Write this percent as a fraction in simplest form and as a decimal.

   _____ and _____

5. Emilio scored 88% on the test. Write this percent as a fraction in simplest form and as a decimal.

   _____ and _____

Lesson 4.2 Comparing and Ordering Percents, Fractions and Decimals

Read the problem carefully and solve. Show your work under each question.

Clarke invests his money in a variety of ways. The portions of his total investment are: 40% in mutual finds, $\frac{1}{4}$ in bonds, 0.15 in stocks, and 20% in real estate. He also owns 3.68 shares of a computer store and $3\frac{4}{5}$ shares of a restaurant.

Helpful Hint

When comparing fractions, decimals, and percents, remember the meaning of each symbol.

>   greater than
<   less than
=   equal to

1. Compare Clarke's investment portions of 40% in mutual funds to $\frac{1}{4}$ in bonds. Use <, >, or =.

   _____

2. Compare Clarke's 3.68 shares in the computer store to the $3\frac{4}{5}$ shares in the restaurant. Use <, >, or =.

   _____

3. Compare Clarke's $\frac{1}{4}$ investment in bonds to his 0.15 investment in stocks. Use <, >, or =.

   _____

4. Order the following from least to greatest. 40%, $3\frac{4}{5}$, 3.68

   _____

5. Order the following from least to greatest: $\frac{11}{10}$, $1\frac{1}{4}$, 1.111, 105%.

   _____

Lesson 4.3 Percent to Fraction and Fraction to Percent

Read the problem carefully and solve. Show your work under each question.

Byron paints shells he collected. He paints 8% of the shells yellow, $\frac{7}{20}$ of the shells purple, 22% of the shells blue, $\frac{1}{4}$ of the shells green, and 10% of the shells red.

Helpful Hint

Percent to fraction:

$40\% = 40 \times \frac{1}{100} = \frac{40}{100} = \frac{2}{5}$

Fraction to percent:

$\frac{1}{4} \times \frac{25}{25} = \frac{25}{100} = 25\%$

1. What is 8% written as a fraction in simplest form?

_____

2. What is $\frac{7}{20}$ written as a percent?

_____

3. What is 22% written as a fraction in simplest form?

_____

4. What is $\frac{1}{2}$ written as a percent?

_____

5. Byron wants to sell the shells and make a profit of 125%. What is 125% written as a fraction in lowest terms?

_____

Lesson 4.4   Percent to Decimal and Decimal to Percent

Read the problem carefully and solve. Show your work under each question.

Kennan grows many different kinds of plants in his backyard. He has a tomato plant, a sunflower, a rose bush, a daisy, and a hosta. He keeps a record of their growth over time.

Helpful Hint

Percent to decimal:
25% = 25 x 0.01 = 0.25

Decimal to percent:
0.73 = 0.73 x 100 = 73%

3. Kennan's rose bush had a growth rate of 0.06 in one week. Write 0.06 as a percent.

_____

1. Kennan's tomato plant grew 12% in one week. Write 12% as a decimal.

_____

4. The daisy grew 2% in one week. Write 2% as a decimal.

_____

2. The sunflower had a growth rate of 0.58 in one month. Write 0.58 as a percent.

_____

5. Kennan recorded that the hosta grew 62% in one month. Write 62% as a decimal.

_____

Lesson 4.5 Finding the Percent of a Number

Read the problem carefully and solve. Show your work under each question.

Jai loves to read. He owns 60 books. The different types of books he owns are action, mystery, sports, literature, and non-fiction.

Helpful Hint

To find a percent of a number, express the percent as a fraction or a decimal and multiply.

1. Of the books Jai owns, 15% are action books. How many action books does he own?

_____

2. The percentage of Jai's books that are mystery is 20%. How many mystery books does he own?

_____

3. Sports books make up 10% of the books Jai owns. How many sports books does he own?

_____

4. Of Jai's books, 30% are classic literature books. How many classic literature books does he own?

_____

5. Jai looked on the library computer to find that there are 600 poetry books. Of the poetry books, $8\frac{1}{2}$% are for children. How many poetry books at the library are for children?

_____

Check What You Learned

Finding Percents

Read the problem carefully and solve. Show your work under each question.

Bill's family owns a hardware store. He orders supplies for the store each month.

1. Bill orders 14% of the paint for the store from one supplier. Write 14% as a decimal.

    _____

2. Bill orders nails in two lengths, $\frac{5}{8}$ inches and 0.62 inches. Compare these lengths using <, >, or =.

    _____

3. Bill orders 135% more kitchen supplies this month than he ordered last month. Write 135% as a fraction in simplest form.

    _____

4. Write the following numbers in order from least to greatest: 0.44, 4%, $\frac{3}{4}$

    _____

5. Bill needs to determine which parts of his inventory take up the most space. Four items are represented by $\frac{11}{8}$, $1\frac{1}{4}$, 1.3, $13\frac{1}{2}$%. Order these amounts from least to greatest.

    _____

6. In July, Bill orders 150 cans of paint. 28% of the order was for white paint. How many cans of white paint did he order?

    _____ cans

NAME _____

 Check What You Know

Calculating Interest

Read the problem carefully and solve. Show your work under each question.

Mr. Gladd wants to take out a loan for $1,500. He researches options at several banks for taking out a $1,500 loan with simple interest.

1. Bank A will give Mr. Gladd a loan for $1,500 at a rate of 8% interest for one year. How much interest will he pay for the loan?

   _____

4. Bank C will give Mr. Gladd a loan for $1,500 at a rate of 7% interest for 5 years. How much interest will he pay for the loan?

   _____

2. Bank A also offers a rate of 6% for a loan that is repaid within 6 months. How much interest would Mr. Gladd pay for this loan?

   _____

5. If Mr. Gladd decides to go with Bank C, what is the total amount that will be repaid to the bank?

   _____

3. Bank B will give Mr. Gladd a loan for $1,500 at a rate of $6\frac{1}{2}$% interest for 3 years. If he goes with this option, what is the total amount that will be repaid to the bank?

   _____

6. Bank D will give Mr. Gladd a loan for $1,500 at a rate of $5\frac{1}{2}$% interest for 2 years. If he goes with this option, what is the total amount that will be repaid to the bank?

   _____

Lesson 5.1 Simple Interest for One Year

Read the problem carefully and solve. Show your work under each question.

Five people each have an amount of money they plan to deposit in saving accounts with simple interest rates.

Helpful Hint

Simple interest (*I*) is determined by multiplying the amount of money (principal, or *p*) by the rate of interest (*r*) by the number of years (time or *t*).

$$I = prt$$

---

1. Abe has $550 to deposit at a rate of 3%. What is the interest earned after one year?

_____

2. Jessi deposits $615 at an interest rate of 5%. What is the interest earned after one year?

_____

3. Heath has $418 and deposits it at an interest rate of 2%. What is the interest after one year?

_____

4. Pablo deposits $825.50 at an interest rate of 4%. What is the interest earned after one year?

_____

5. Kami deposits $1,140 at an interest rate of 6%. What is the interest earned after one year?

_____

Lesson 5.2 Simple Interest for More Than One Year

Read the problem carefully and solve. Show your work under each question.

Abe, Jessi, Heath, Pablo, and Kami all decide to leave their money in their savings accounts for more than one year at a simple interest rate.

Helpful Hint

Remember to substitute the number of years into the simple interest formula. The total amount in the account is the interest earned plus the initial deposit.

1. Abe deposited $550 at the simple interest rate of 3%. How much money will he have in the account after 7 years?

   _____

2. Jessi deposited $615 at the simple interest rate of 5%. How much money will she have in the account after 3 years?

   _____

3. Heath deposited $418 at the simple interest rate of 2%. How much money will he have in the account after $5\frac{1}{2}$ years?

   _____

4. Pablo deposited $825.50 at the simple interest rate of 4%. How much money will he have in the account after 8 years?

   _____

5. Kami deposited $1,140 at the simple interest rate of 6%. How much money will she have in the account after 4 years?

   _____

Lesson 5.3 Simple Interest for Less Than One Year

Read the problem carefully and solve. Show your work under each question.

A group of people is looking to borrow money for renovations on the community center. Each person looks at the simple interest rate of a different bank for part of the project.

Helpful Hint
Convert fractions to decimals before calculating the interest.

1. Jaden can get a $375 loan at $5\frac{1}{2}$% interest for $\frac{1}{2}$ year. What is the total amount of money that will be paid back to the bank?

   _____

2. Gabe can get a $1,500 loan at 3% for $\frac{1}{4}$ year. What is the total amount of money that will be paid back to the bank?

   _____

3. Keisha can get a $2,600 loan at $4\frac{1}{2}$% for $\frac{1}{2}$ year. What is the total amount of money that will be paid back to the bank?

   _____

4. Donna can get an $850 loan at 6% for $\frac{3}{4}$ year. What is the total amount of money that will be paid back to the bank?

   _____

5. Leo can get an $800 loan at 8% for $\frac{1}{4}$ year. What is the total amount of money that will be paid back to the bank?

   _____

Check What You Learned

Calculating Interest

Read the problem carefully and solve. Show your work under each question.

Caroline looks at several different ways that she can invest $5,000. She wants to get the greatest possible return on her investment.

1. Caroline considers buying a certificate of deposit for $5,000 that pays $5\frac{1}{2}$% simple interest for 1 year. How much money will she earn in interest?

_____

2. If Caroline buys the certificate of deposit described in Question 1, how much money will she have in total after 3 months?

_____

3. Caroline considers investing $5,000 in a savings account that pays 3% simple interest for 8 years. How much money will she have in total after 8 years?

_____

4. Caroline considers buying a certificate of deposit for $5,000 that pays 7% simple interest for 5 years. How much money will she earn in interest after 5 years?

_____

5. If Caroline buys a certificate of deposit for $5,000 at a simple interest rate of 5%, how much interest will be earned after $5\frac{1}{2}$ years?

_____

6. If Caroline invests $5,000 in an investment account that pays $4\frac{1}{2}$% simple interest for 3 years, how much money will she have at the end of the 3 years?

_____

Mid-Test Chapters 1–5

Read the problem carefully and solve. Show your work under each question.

Company A sold 683,400 golf balls last year. Company B sold 872,300 golf balls last year. Company A sells golf balls in packs of 3 and Company B sells golf balls in packs of 4. In one month, Blair uses $3\frac{2}{3}$ packs of golf balls from Company A and $2\frac{1}{2}$ packs of golf balls from company B.

1. How many golf balls did companies A and B sell altogether last year?

_____

2. How many more golf balls did Company B sell than Company A?

_____

3. Company A plans to sell 4 times as many golf balls this year than it did last year. How many golf balls does it plan to sell this year?

_____

4. How many packs of golf balls did Company A sell?

_____

5. How many golf balls did Blair use from Company A in the month?

_____

6. Blair used $3\frac{2}{3}$ packs of Company A golf balls per month. If he used $29\frac{1}{3}$ packs of golf balls, how many months did this cover?

_____ months

Mid-Test Chapters 1–5

Read the problem carefully and solve. Show your work under each question.

Crystal is making bread at her bakery job. She has 15.6 pounds of white dough and 22.4 pounds of wheat dough.

1. How many total pounds of dough does Crystal have?

_____ pounds

2. How many more pounds of wheat dough does she have than white dough?

_____ pounds

3. Crystal makes mini baguettes with the white dough. If each baguette weighs 0.3 pound, how many baguettes can she make?

_____ baguettes

4. Crystal needs to record the amount of dough she uses every day. The amounts she uses need to be recorded as fractions. How much dough for wheat bread does Crystal have, written as an improper fraction in simplest form?

_____

5. For her next batch, Crystal orders 2.55 times as many pounds of wheat dough than she has now. How many pounds of wheat dough does she order?

_____ pounds

6. Last week, Crystal used 51.761 pounds of dough to make biscuits. If it takes 0.0955 pound of dough per biscuit, how many biscuits did Crystal make?

_____ biscuits

Mid-Test Chapters 1–5

Read the problem carefully and solve. Show your work under each question.

Ken wants to invest $8,000 he has saved over the last few years. He distributes his money into different types of investments.

---

1. Ken deposits $360 into a savings account with a simple interest rate of $6\frac{1}{4}$%. How much money will he have after 1 year?

_____

2. How much money will be in Ken's savings account after $3\frac{1}{2}$ years?

_____

3. Ken invests $1,200 into a fund with a simple interest rate of 5%. How much will be in the account after 9 months?

_____

4. Ken invested $2,300 in a 3-year CD with a simple interest rate. After 3 years, Ken had $2,472.50. What was the interest rate?

_____

5. Ken invested $19\frac{3}{4}$ % of his $8,000 in part-ownership of a store. How much did he invest?

_____

6. Ken's cousin India also invested some money. India's total investments were 115% Ken's $8,000 investment. How much money did India invest?

_____

Mid-Test Chapters 1–5

Read the problem carefully and solve. Show your work under each question.

Ava works for a house-painting company. She uses scale drawings to buy paint for the houses and to plan the work.

1. Ava finds that 3 out of every 5 houses the company paints are white. If they paint 20 houses, how many are white?

   _____

2. It took 8 quarts of paint to paint 2 sides of a garage. If the 3rd side is the same size as each of the first 2 sides, how much paint will it take to paint 3 sides of the garage?

   _____ quarts

3. Two windows on the house have 18 total panes of glass. How many panes of glass are there for 7 windows?

   _____

4. A scale drawing of one house has a scale of 2 inches = 3 feet. The drawing of the house is 18 inches high. What is the actual height of the house?

   _____ feet

5. The scale drawing on another house has a scale of 4 inches = 16 feet. If the actual house is 36 feet high, how tall is the drawing of the house?

   _____ inches

6. On a map with a scale of 3 inches = 9 miles, Ava's house is 10 inches from her workplace. How many miles does Ava live from her workplace?

   _____ miles

Check What You Know

Ratio and Proportion

Read the problem carefully and solve. Show your work under each question.

William is a real estate developer. He plans to build a mall.

1. Four out of 100 parking spaces in the lot will be near elevators. If there are 1,225 parking spaces in all, how many spaces will be near elevators?

_____

4. In the food court area of the mall, 1 out of every 4 restaurants will be for healthy-choice foods. If there are 3 healthy-choice restaurants in the food court, how many restaurants are there in all?

_____

2. One out of every 4 exits will be an emergency exit. If there are 88 exits at the mall, how many are emergency exits?

_____

5. A scale drawing for a store in the mall has a ratio of 2 inches = 5 feet. If the width of the store on the drawing is 8 inches, what is the width of the actual store?

_____ feet

3. William wants 2 out of every 3 stores in the mall to be clothing stores. If there are 150 stores in the mall, how many stores will be clothing stores?

_____

6. A scale drawing for a window in the mall has a ratio of 2 inches = 4 feet. If the width of the window on the drawing is 3 inches, what is the width of the actual window?

_____ feet

Lesson 6.1 Ratio and Proportion

Read the problem carefully and solve. Show your work under each question.

Mrs. Ryan writes several ratios on the whiteboard. Students are asked to write or identify equal ratios. Ratios that are equal are proportions and represented by an equal sign.

Helpful Hint

A proportion is a statement that two ratios are equal. In a proportion, the cross products of the terms are equal.

1. The ratios $\frac{4}{7}$ and $\frac{16}{28}$ are written on the whiteboard. Are the ratios equal?

    _____

2. The ratios $\frac{3}{5}$ and $\frac{15}{30}$ are written on the whiteboard. Are the ratios equal?

    _____

3. The ratios $\frac{2}{4}$ and $\frac{3}{6}$ are written on the whiteboard. Do the ratios form a proportion?

    _____

4. The ratios $\frac{16}{9}$ and $\frac{48}{27}$ are written on the whiteboard. Do the ratios form a proportion?

    _____

5. The ratios $\frac{4}{24}$ and $\frac{?}{30}$ are written on the whiteboard. Which number can be inserted to make the ratios equal?

    _____

Lesson 6.2 Solving Proportion Problems

Read the problem carefully and solve. Show your work under each question.

Mr. Dolby is in charge of ordering supplies for his school. Each month, he takes inventory of the supplies.

Helpful Hint

To set up a proportion problem, use a variable to represent the missing number. Then, cross-multiply and solve for the variable.

1. There are 64 pencils in 4 boxes. How many additional pencils will there be when Mr. Dolby orders 8 more boxes?

    _____

2. Mr. Dolby finds that 3 out of every 8 highlighters are yellow. If there are 64 highlighters in all, how many of them are yellow?

    _____

3. There are 96 reams of paper in 12 boxes of paper. How many reams of paper are there in 16 boxes of paper?

    _____

4. There are 90 pens in 5 boxes. Mr. Dolby needs 216 more pens. How many boxes will he order?

    _____

5. There are 42 notebooks in 3 boxes. If there are 7 boxes of notebooks, how many notebooks are there in all?

    _____

Lesson 6.3 Proportions and Scale Drawings

Read the problem carefully and solve. Show your work under each question.

Denise works for the city planning department. She is an architect. Denise often uses scale drawings to represent buildings, parks, bridges, and other real objects in the city.

Helpful Hint

Remember to keep the units in the same parts of the proportion. For example, if yards are the denominator of the first ratio, then yards should be in the denominator of the other ratio.

1. A map of the city uses a scale of 2 inches = 8 miles. If the city is 24 miles wide, how wide is the city on the map?

   _____ inches

2. A bridge is 68 feet long. A scale drawing of the bridge has a ratio of 1 inch = 17 feet. How long is the drawing of the bridge?

   _____ inches

3. A scale drawing of a city park uses a scale of 3 inches = 9 feet. If the width of the park on the drawing is 9 inches, how wide is the actual park?

   _____ feet

4. A scale drawing of the new city hall building uses a scale of 2 inches = 7 feet. If the height of the building on the drawing is 36 inches, how tall is the actual building?

   _____ feet

5. A library is 75 feet long. A scale drawing of the library has a ratio of 3 inches = 15 feet. How long is the library in the drawing?

   _____ inches

Check What You Learned

Ratio and Proportion

Read the problem carefully and solve. Show your work under each question.

Barry works for an architectural design firm. His latest project involves the construction of a condominium building.

1. Barry designs the layout of the parking garage for the condominium building. For each condo, Barry plans for 2 parking spaces. If there are 125 condo units, how many parking spaces are there?

   _____

2. For every 10 rooms, 4 will have carpeted flooring. If there are 350 total rooms in the building, how many will have carpeted flooring?

   _____

3. Three out of every 5 condominium units will have a balcony. If there are 125 condo units, how many condos will have a balcony?

   _____

4. One floor of the building will have 27 condominium units. If 2 out of every 9 units on this floor are next to a stairwell, how many units will be near a stairwell?

   _____

5. A scale drawing for a bedroom in the building has a ratio of 2 inches = 6 feet. If the width of the bedroom on the drawing is 3 inches, what is the width of the actual bedroom?

   _____ feet

6. A scale drawing for the lobby of the building has a ratio of 8 centimeters = 24 feet. If the width of the lobby on the drawing is 12 centimeters, what is the width of the actual lobby?

   _____ feet

NAME _____

Check What You Know

Customary Measurement

Read the problem carefully and solve. Show your work under each question.

Emma spends 14 days at summer camp. The camp is on a 4.2–mile stretch of a lake. Emma swims every day while at camp.

1. Emma's bag packed with clothing and personal items for camp weighs 26.5 pounds. How many ounces does her bag weigh?

   _____ ounces

2. The camp sits on a 4.2–mile stretch of the lake. What is this distance in yards?

   _____ yards

3. Emma swims for 195 minutes in the first week. How many hours does she swim?

   _____ hours

4. How many seconds did Emma swim during the first week of camp?

   _____ seconds

5. Emma brings a water bottle to camp that holds 2.5 pints of water. How many quarts of water does the bottle hold?

   _____ quarts

6. One day, Emma fills her water bottle with lemonade. How many cups of lemonade are in the bottle?

   _____ cups

Lesson 7.1 Units of Length (inches, feet, yards, and miles)

Read the problem carefully and solve. Show your work under each question.

Amira lives 5.3 miles from school. Her house is 45 feet away from the house next door and 243 feet from her cousin's house. She also lives 124 yards from the local market.

Helpful Hint

Use the table and multiply or divide to convert units of measure.
1 foot (ft.) = 12 inches (in.)
1 yard (yd.) = 3 ft. = 36 in.
1 mile (mi.) = 1,760 yd. = 5,280 ft.

1. How many feet does Amira live from school?

_____ feet

2. What is the distance, in yards, between Amira's house and school?

_____ yards

3. How many inches does Amira live from the house next door?

_____ inches

4. How many yards does Amira live from her cousin's house?

_____ yards

5. How many inches does Amira live from the local market?

_____ inches

Lesson 7.2 Liquid Volume (cups, pints, quarts, gallons)

Read the problem carefully and solve. Show your work under each question.

Chris plans for a brunch. He has a pitcher that holds 2 quarts of liquid. He buys 3 gallons of iced tea. He also buys 0.75 gallon of tomato juice and makes 6 pints of soup.

Helpful Hint

Use the table and multiply or divide to convert units of measure.
1 pint (pt.) = 2 cups (c.)
1 quart (qt.) = 2 pt. = 4 c.
1 gallon (gal.) = 4 qt. = 8 pt. = 16 c.

1. Chris fills the pitcher with orange juice. How many cups of orange juice are in the pitcher?

   _____ cups

2. How many cups of iced tea did Chris buy?

   _____ cups

3. How many quarts of iced tea did Chris buy?

   _____ quarts

4. How many pints of tomato juice did Chris buy?

   _____ pints

5. How many cups of soup did Chris make?

   _____ cups

Lesson 7.3 Weight (ounces, pounds, tons)

Read the problem carefully and solve. Show your work under each question.

Carla wants to know the weight of different objects. She finds that her dad's truck weighs 1.13 tons. Her dog weighs 42.6 pounds. Carla's couch weighs 158 pounds and her camera weighs 1.2 pounds.

> **Helpful Hint**
>
> Use the table and multiply or divide to convert units of measure.
> 1 pound (lb.) = 16 ounces (oz.)
> 1 ton (T.) = 2,000 lb. = 32,000 oz.

1. How many pounds does the truck weigh?

_____ pounds

2. How many ounces does Carla's dog weigh?

_____ ounces

3. Carla wants to convert the weight of her couch into tons. What is the weight of her couch in tons?

_____ ton

4. How many ounces does the truck weigh?

_____ ounces

5. How many ounces does Carla's camera weigh?

_____ ounces

Lesson 7.4 Time

Read the problem carefully and solve. Show your work under each question.

Brad records the amount of time to do certain things. It takes him 2.3 hours to complete his homework. It takes him 135 seconds to brush his teeth. He usually sleeps 9 hours each night. He spent $13\frac{1}{2}$ days on vacation last year.

Helpful Hint

Use the table and multiply or divide to convert units of measure.

1 minute (min.) = 60 seconds (sec.)
1 hour (hr.) = 60 min. = 3,600 sec.
1 day = 24 hr. = 1,440 min.

3. What is the amount of time, in days and hours, that Brad sleeps in a week?

_____ days _____ hours

1. How many minutes does it take for Brad to do his homework?

_____ minutes

4. How many hours did Brad spend on vacation last year?

_____ hours

2. How many minutes does it take for Brad to brush his teeth?

_____ minutes

5. How many minutes did Brad spend on vacation last year?

_____ minutes

Check What You Learned

Customary Measurement

Read the problem carefully and solve. Show your work under each question.

Harry takes an art class. The class meets for 18 sessions and each session is 75 minutes. The art class is 0.5 mile from Harry's house.

---

1. In class, Harry makes a sculpture that weighs 73.6 pounds. How many tons does the sculpture weigh?

_____ ton

4. How many seconds is each art class?

_____ seconds

2. How many inches is Harry's house from the art class?

_____ inches

5. Harry adds 3 cups of water to his clay to make it softer. What is this amount of water expressed as quarts?

_____ quart

3. How many hours long is each art class?

_____ hours

6. Harry added 4.5 pints of water to another batch of clay. How many cups of water is this?

_____ cups

NAME _____

Check What You Know

Metric Measurement

Read the problem carefully and solve. Show your work under each question.

Drew needs containers for storage. He buys a shipping box that has a length of 150 centimeters and a width of 0.55 meter. The box can hold up to 28 kilograms of weight. Drew also buys a large plastic bin that can hold up to 83.2 liters of liquid.

1. Drew wants to find out how many kiloliters the large plastic bin can hold. Convert 83.2 liters to kiloliters.

_____ kiloliter

4. How many metric tons can the shipping box hold?

_____ metric ton

2. Drew has 7,050 milliliters of punch that he wants to put in the plastic bin. He converts the amount to liters to see if it will fit in the bin. What is 7,050 milliliters written in liters?

_____ liters

5. How many kilometers wide is the box?

_____ kilometer

3. Drew's mother asks him how many grams the box can hold. How many grams does he tell her?

_____ grams

6. Drew calculates the length of the box in millimeters. How many millimeters in length is the box?

_____ millimeters

Lesson 8.1 Units of Length (millimeters, centimeters, meters, and kilometers)

Read the problem carefully and solve. Show your work under each question.

Addie lives 12 kilometers from her grandmother's house and 266 meters from a gas station. She makes a gift for her grandmother using 450 millimeters of ribbon and 38 centimeters of yarn.

Helpful Hint

1 centimeter (cm) = 10 millimeters (mm)
1 meter (m) = 100 cm = 1,000 mm
1 kilometer (km) = 1,000 m

1 mm = 0.1 cm = 0.001 m
1 cm = 0.01 m
1 m = 0.001 km

1. Addie visits her grandmother on her birthday. How many meters away is her grandmother's house?

   _____ meters

2. Addie wants to know how many centimeters of ribbon she used to make her grandmother's gift. How many centimeters of ribbon did she use?

   _____ centimeters

3. Addie decides to calculate the distance from her house to the gas station in millimeters. Find the distance in millimeters.

   _____ millimeters

4. How many meters of yarn does Addie use to make the gift for her grandmother?

   _____ meter

5. Addie wants to know how many centimeters she lives from her grandmother's house. Write 12 kilometers as centimeters.

   _____ centimeters

Lesson 8.2 Liquid Volume (milliliters, liters, and kiloliters)

Read the problem carefully and solve. Show your work under each question.

Travis likes chemistry and often sets up his own experiments for fun. During one experiment he has 3.5 liters of orange juice, 55 milliliters of seltzer water, 0.007 kiloliter of cranberry juice, and 22.4 liters of ginger ale.

Helpful Hint

1 liter (L) = 1,000 milliliters (mL)
1 kiloliter (kL) = 1,000 liters

1 mL = 0.001 m
1 liter = 0.001 kL

1. How many liters of cranberry juice does Travis have?

_____ liters

2. How many liters of orange juice and cranberry juice does he have in all?

_____ liters

3. Travis's sister asks him how many milliliters of ginger ale he has. Write the volume of ginger ale in milliliters.

_____ milliliters

4. How many liters of seltzer water does Travis have?

_____ liter

5. Travis measures the orange juice in milliliters as part of the experiment. How many milliliters of orange juice does he have?

_____ milliliters

Lesson 8.3 Weight (milligrams, grams, kilograms, and metric tons)

Read the problem carefully and solve. Show your work under each question.

Cole completes a project on the weight mass of various items within his community. He researches and records the weight of many types of items for the project.

Helpful Hint

1 gram (g) = 1,000 milligrams (mg)
1 kilogram (kg) = 1,000 g
1 metric ton (MT) = 1,000 kg

1 mg = 0.001 g
1 g = 0.001 kg
1 kg = 0.001 MT

1. A box of crackers at the store weighs 0.84 kilogram. Cole converts the weight to grams. What is the weight of the box of crackers in grams?

   _____ grams

2. The town dump has 42,000,000 kilograms of garbage. What is this weight in metric tons?

   _____ metric tons

3. A meal at the local diner has 2.7 grams of sodium. Cole wants to know this amount in milligrams. Rewrite 2.7 grams in milligrams.

   _____ milligrams

4. A chair at a furniture store weighs 11 kilograms. What is the weight of the chair in metric tons?

   _____ metric ton

5. A frozen entree from the market weighs 326 grams. Cole rewrites this weight in milligrams. How many milligrams does the entree weigh?

   _____ milligrams

Check What You Learned

Metric Measurement

Read the problem carefully and solve. Show your work under each question.

Fiona works for a delivery service. The delivery truck is 16.4 meters in length. The truck can hold 0.5 metric ton of cargo. There is a separate container in the truck for liquids. This container can hold up to 2,100 liters.

CHAPTER 8 POSTTEST

1. Fiona wants the truck to deliver 1.8 kiloliters of a cleaning fluid to a customer. What is 1.8 kiloliters written as liters?

   _____ liters

2. How many milliliters of liquid can the container hold?

   _____ milliliters

3. Fiona wants to know how many kilograms of cargo the truck can hold, so she can notify a customer. How many kilograms of cargo can the truck hold?

   _____ kilograms

4. Fiona has a customer that has a large shipment measured in grams. How many grams can the truck hold?

   _____ grams

5. Fiona calculates the length of the truck in kilometers. How many kilometers in length is the truck?

   _____ kilometer

6. How many millimeters long is the truck?

   _____ millimeters

Check What You Know

Probability and Statistics

Read the problem carefully and solve. Show your work under each question.

Carter asks 40 of his friends what their favorite type of music is. He records the data on paper and then makes a circle graph to display the results. The circle graph is shown to the right.

Favorite Type of Music

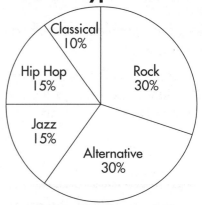

40 people responded

1. How many people said they like Rock music as their favorite?

   _____ people

2. Carter compares the data for each person he interviewed. Which two types of music account for three-fifths of the people interviewed?

   _____

3. How many people like Hip Hop music as their favorite?

   _____ people

4. How many people from Carter's survey chose Jazz or Classical as their favorite type of music?

   _____ people

5. If the number of people who chose Rock tripled, how many people would have chosen Rock music?

   _____ people

6. When Carter was giving his report in school, he was asked how many people chose Alternative, Jazz, or Classical. How did Carter respond?

   _____ people

NAME _____

Check What You Know

Probability and Statistics

Read the problem carefully and solve. Show your work under each question.

Marisa tracks the rainfall each month for March, April, May, and June. She records the data and then makes a histogram to display the data. The histogram is shown to the right.

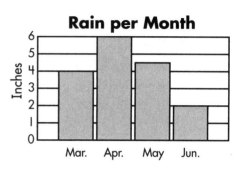

Rain per Month

1. Marisa looks to the graph to see how many inches of rain fell in May. How many inches of rain fell in May?

   _____ inches

2. How many more inches did it rain in April than in March?

   _____ inches

3. Marisa shows the histogram to her dad. Her dad wants Marisa to tell him how many inches it rained in all 4 months. How many inches did it rain altogether?

   _____ inches

4. Last year, it rained 4 more inches in June than it rained this year. How many inches did it rain in June last year?

   _____ inches

5. Marisa wants to know how many inches it would have rained in April if two less inches of rain had fallen than she recorded. How many inches of rain would there have been?

   _____ inches

6. Marisa brings her histogram to school. Her teacher asks her how many more inches it rained in April than it did in June. What did she say?

   _____ inches

Lesson 9.1 Bar Graphs

Read the problem carefully and solve. Show your work under each question.

Ivan created a survey to find out the favorite sports of the boys and girls in his grade at school. With the results, he drew the graph to the right.

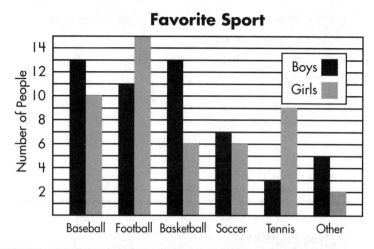

Favorite Sport

Helpful Hint

Use the key given in a double-bar graph to help you identify the numbers of boys and girls who identified each favorite sport.

1. How many people responded to the survey in all?

   _____ people

2. Ivan compares the number of boys who chose basketball to the number of boys who chose football. How many more boys chose basketball than football?

   _____ boys

3. Ivan calculates how many girls chose either soccer or other as their answer for the survey. How many girls chose either soccer or other as an option on the survey?

   _____ girls

4. How many total people chose basketball as their favorite sport?

   _____ people

5. Ivan compares the number of girls who chose football to the number of girls who chose soccer. How many more girls chose football than soccer?

   _____ girls

Lesson 9.2 Histograms

Read the problem carefully and solve. Show your work under each question.

Iman gave a survey to his English class to find out how many hours each student spends reading each week. He graphed the data using the histogram shown to the right.

Number of Hours Spent Reading per Week

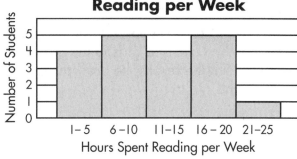

Helpful Hint

Each bar in the histogram represents an interval of 5 hours. The intervals are equal and the bars represent continuous data.

1. Iman wants to know how many students read between 16 and 25 hours per week. How many students read between 16 and 25 hours per week?

   _____ students

2. How many more students read between 16 to 20 hours per week than read between 11 to 15 hours per week?

   _____ student

3. If the survey represents every student in the English class, how many students are there in this class?

   _____ students

4. Iman calculates the number of students that read between 11 and 20 hours per week. How many students read between 11 and 20 hours per week?

   _____ students

5. How many more students read between 11 and 15 hours per week than read between 21 and 25 hours per week?

   _____ students

Lesson 9.3 Line Graphs

Read the problem carefully and solve. Show your work under each question.

James plays offense on a hockey team. He keeps track of his performance for the first 10 games of the season. He then graphs the data in the line graph shown to the right.

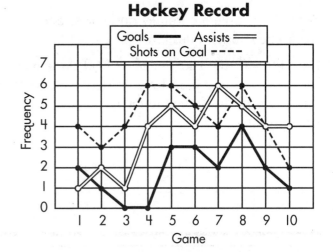

Hockey Record

Helpful Hint

Use the key shown in the graph to properly read which line represents goals, assists, and shots on goal.

1. During which game did James have the most assists?

game _____

2. James calculates his total shots on goal. How many shots on goal did he have in the 10 games in all?

_____ shots on goal

3. During which games did James get 2 goals?

games _____

4. How many more assists did James have in game 7 than in game 2?

_____ assists

5. James analyzes his goals for the 10 games. During which games did he have zero goals?

games _____

Lesson 9.4 Circle Graphs

NAME _____

Read the problem carefully and solve. Show your work under each question.

Destini conducts a survey of all 800 students in her school to find their favorite berry. She graphs the results of the survey in the circle graph shown to the right.

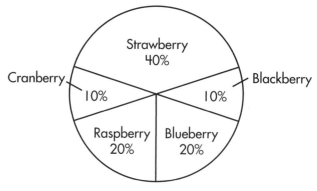

Favorite Berry

Helpful Hint

Each sector shows the percent of people who prefer each berry.

The circle is divided into sectors that add up to 100%. Each sector represents a percentage of the total number of people.

---

1. Destini says that two berries together account for one-fifth of the people surveyed. Which two berries together total one-fifth of the people in the survey?

   _____ and _____

2. Destini calculates how many people prefer blackberries. How many people prefer blackberries?

   _____ people

3. How many people prefer either cranberries or strawberries?

   _____ people

4. How many people prefer blueberries?

   _____ people

Lesson 9.5 Scattergrams

Read the problem carefully and solve. Show your work under each question.

Zoe collects data for a charity walk-a-thon relay. She recorded the number of miles some teams walked and the number of hours they walked. She records the results in the scattergram to the right.

Walk-a-thon Miles

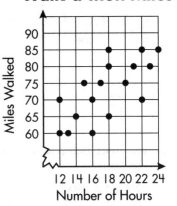

Helpful Hint

A **positive relationship** exists in a scattergram if, as one value increases, the other value increases as well. A **negative relationship** exists in a scattergram if, as one value increases, the other value decreases. If there is no trend to be found in the scattergram, then **no relationship** exists within the data.

1. One team had 20 hours of walking. How many miles did the team walk?

   _____ miles

2. Three teams walked for 18 hours. What were the distances they walked?

   _____ miles

3. How many teams walked more than 75 miles?

   _____

4. How many teams walked for 20 hours or more?

   _____

5. What type of relationship—positive, negative, or none—was there between the number of hours walked and the number of miles walked?

   _____

Lesson 9.6 Measures of Central Tendency

Read the problem carefully and solve. Show your work under each question.

Dave records the outside temperature at noon for seven consecutive days. The temperatures are recorded in the table below.

Monday	Tuesday	Wednesday	Thursday	Friday	Saturday	Sunday
62° F	65° F	75° F	78° F	70° F	77° F	70° F

Helpful Hint

The **mean** is the average of a set of numbers. The **median** is the middle number of a set of numbers that is ordered from least to greatest. The **mode** is the number that appears most often in a set of numbers. The **range** is the difference between the greatest and least numbers in the set.

1. Dave wants to find the median temperature for the week. What is the median temperature for the week?

   _____

2. Dave thought that there were some days that seemed cold and some days that seemed hot. What was the range of the temperatures?

   _____

3. Dave wants to know which temperature occurred the most often during the week, so he finds the mode of the temperatures. What is the mode of the data?

   _____

4. Dave wants to find the mean temperature for the week so he can share it with his classmates. What is the mean temperature for the week?

   _____

5. If the temperature on the 8th day was 55° F, which measure would change the most?

   _____

Lesson 9.7 Stem-and-Leaf Plots

Read the problem carefully and solve. Show your work under each question.

Wren collects information on the ages of the houses in his neighborhood. He decides to display these ages in the stem-and-leaf plot shown to the right.

Stems	Leaves
1	1 3 3 6
2	2 4 7
3	0 3 7 9
4	1 4 9

Key: 4 1 = 41

Helpful Hint

The right column of a stem-and-leaf plot shows the **leaves**—the ones digit of each number. The other digits form the **stems** and are shown in the left column. The **key** explains how to read the plot.

1. After he creates the stem-and-leaf plot, Wren wants to determine the oldest house in his neighborhood. What is the age of the oldest house?

   _____ years

2. What is the age of the newest house in his neighborhood?

   _____ years

3. Wren's father asks him how many houses are between 25 and 35 years old. What is Wren's answer?

   _____ houses

4. Wren's teacher takes a look at the graph. She asks Wren to tell her how many houses are less than 30 years old. What is Wren's response?

   _____ houses

5. What is the mean age of houses in Wren's neighborhood?

   _____ years

Lesson 9.8 Frequency Tables

Read the problem carefully and solve. Show your work under each question.

After giving a test to her class, Mrs. Ling decides to make a frequency table to show the number of hours each student studied for the test. The table is shown below. The actual hours studied were: 6, 10, 2, 4, 5, 7, 9, 8, 3, 6, 8, 11, 7, 1.

Test Scores			
Hours Studied	Frequency	Cumulative Frequency	Relative Frequency
0–1.9	1	1	7.1%
2–3.9	2	3	14.3%
4–5.9	2	5	14.3%
6–7.9	4		28.6%
8–9.9	3	12	
10–11.9	2	14	14.3%

Helpful Hint

A **frequency table** shows how often a range of numbers occurs. **Cumulative frequency** is the total of a frequency and all of the frequencies below it. **Relative frequency** is the percent of a specific category compared to all of the categories.

1. Mrs. Ling wants to know how many of the students studied in the 2–3.9 hours range. How many students were in that range?

    _____ students

2. What was the cumulative frequency for 6–7.9 hours?

    _____ students

3. How many students studied for more than 5.9 hours?

    _____ students

4. What is the total number of students who took the test?

    _____ students

5. What was the relative frequency of students who studied 8–9.9 hours? Round your answer to the nearest tenth of a percent.

    _____ number of hours studied

Lesson 9.9 Line Plots

Read the problem carefully and solve. Show your work under each question.

Antonio conducts a survey to find the number of soccer balls each member of his soccer team owns so players can practice in their neighborhoods on a weeknight. After the survey, he graphs the results using a line plot. The line plot is shown to the right.

Number of Soccer Balls

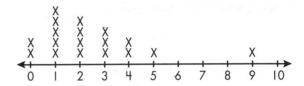

Helpful Hint

A **line plot** is a graph that shows the frequency of data on a number line. Line plots make it easy to identify the mode, range, and any outliers in a data set. **Outliers** are data points that are much larger or smaller than other values.

1. How many team members do not own any soccer balls?

_____ members

2. The coach of the soccer team wants to know how many members of the team have at least 4 soccer balls. How many members is this?

_____ members

3. How many soccer balls are there in all?

_____ soccer balls

4. Antonio compares the members of the team that have only 1 soccer ball with the members of the team that have exactly 5 soccer balls. How many more members have only 1 soccer ball?

_____ members

5. When Antonio shows the line plot he made based on the survey to his coach, the coach asks him what the outlier is for the data. How many soccer balls represent the outlier for the data?

_____ soccer balls

Lesson 9.10 Box-and-Whisker Plots

Read the problem carefully and solve. Show your work under each question.

Ginny interviews 24 of her friends to find the number of movies each friend watched over the summer. After she collects the data, Ginny graphs the results using a box-and-whisker plot. This plot is shown to the right.

Movies Watched Over the Summer

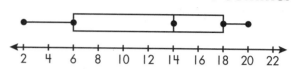

Helpful Hint

A **box-and-whisker plot** displays data along a number line. Quartiles are used to divide the data into four equal parts.

3. How many of Ginny's friends watched between 14 and 18 movies?

_____ friends

1. What is the median number of movies watched?

_____ movies watched

4. What percent of Ginny's friends watched between 6 and 18 movies?

_____ percent

2. What is most number of movies watched by a student?

_____ movies watched

5. What is the lower quartile for the data?

_____ movies watched

Lesson 9.11 Tree Diagrams

Read the problem carefully and solve. Show your work under each question.

Cody is doing an experiment with a penny and a cube with sides numbered from 1–6. He wants to draw a tree diagram to show the sample space for all the possible outcomes (possible results) for tossing a penny and rolling the number cube at the same time.

Helpful Hint

A **sample space** is a set of all possible outcomes for an activity or experiment. To determine the sample space, it is helpful to organize the possibilities using a list, chart, picture, or tree diagram.

1. Make a tree diagram to show all of the possible outcomes.

2. How many possible outcomes are there?

   _____ possible outcomes

3. In how many possible outcomes does the penny land on heads?

   _____ outcomes

4. How many possible outcomes involve rolling a number less than 5?

   _____ outcomes

5. Cody found a spinner with 3 equal sections. How many possible outcomes are there for flipping the coin, rolling the number cube, and spinning the spinner all at the same time?

   _____ outcomes

Lesson 9.12 Calculating Probability

Read the problem carefully and solve. Show your work under each question.

Luis has a box of different colored markers. The box contains 4 red markers, 6 blue markers, 3 purple markers, 2 green markers, and 1 black marker.

Helpful Hint

An **outcome** is any of the possible results of an activity or experiment. **Probability** is the likelihood that a specific outcome or set of outcomes will occur. Probability is the ratio of desired outcome(s) to the sample space. It can be expressed as a ratio, fraction, decimal, or percent.

1. What is the probability that a red marker is randomly chosen from the box? Write your answer as a fraction in simplest form.

_____

2. What is the probability of randomly choosing a purple marker from the box? Write your answer as a ratio.

_____

3. What is the probability of randomly choosing a green marker out of the box? Write your answer as a decimal.

_____

4. What is the probability of randomly choosing a yellow marker? Write your answer as a percent.

_____

5. What is the probability of randomly choosing either a blue or green marker from the box? Write your answer as a percent.

_____

Check What You Learned

Probability and Statistics

Read the problem carefully and solve. Show your work under each question.

Nathan takes a survey to find out how many hours per week the 20 people in his guitar class practice playing guitar. He displays the results in a circle graph shown to the right.

Hours of Guitar Practice Per Week

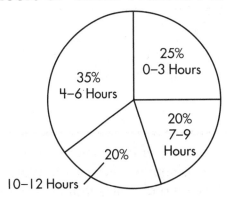

20 people responded.

1. Nathan writes down how many people practice guitar 4–6 hours per week. How many people does he write down?

   _____ people

2. Nathan is asked how many more people practice 0–3 hours per week than practice 7–9 hours per week. What is his answer?

   _____

3. How many people practice guitar either 4–6 hours per week or 7–9 hours per week?

   _____ people

4. Nathan's cousin is one of the people surveyed who practice 0–3 hours per week. How many other people practice 0–3 hours per week?

   _____ people

5. How many more people practice 4–6 hours per week than 7–9 hours per week?

   _____ people

6. If the number of people who practice 10–12 hours per week doubles, how many people would then practice 10–12 hours per week?

   _____ people

Check What You Learned

Probability and Statistics

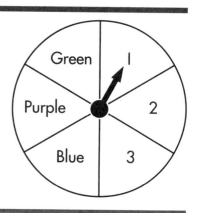

Read the problem carefully and solve. Show your work under each question.

Callista likes to make her own probability experiments. She decides to make the spinner shown to the right for an experiment.

1. Callista wants to know the probability that the spinner will land on a color. What is the probability that the spinner will land on a color? Write your answer as a decimal.

   _____

2. Callista hopes that the spinner will land on an odd number. What is the probability that the spinner will land on an odd number? Write your answer as a ratio in simplest form.

   _____

3. Callista has a friend that wants to know the probability that the spinner will land on either an even number or a color. What is the probability? Show your answer as a fraction in simplest form.

   _____

4. Callista hopes that the spinner will land on the number 2. What is the probability that the spinner will land on the number 2? Write your answer as a fraction.

   _____

5. Callista wants to know the probability that the spinner will land on any section except the color green. Write your answer as a percent rounded to the nearest tenth.

   _____

6. What is the probability that the spinner will land on any number or the color blue? Write your answer as a decimal rounded to the nearest tenth.

   _____

Check What You Know

Geometry

Read the problem carefully and solve. Show your work under each question.

Dawn drew the figure to the right for an art class. In the class, she is studying various angles that can be used when she draws or paints. She also learns about various geometric figures in the art class.

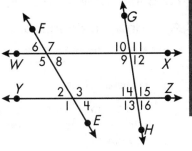

---

1. Dawn measures angle 8. What is the measure of angle 8?

   _____

2. How would Dawn identify the ray that starts at point Z and passes through point Y?

   _____

3. Dawn looks at the drawing to classify the angle represented by the number 4. Is angle 4 obtuse, right, or acute?

   _____

4. In Dawn's drawing, $\overleftrightarrow{WX}$ and $\overleftrightarrow{YZ}$ are parallel. If the measure of angle 11 is 110°, what is the measure of angle 10?

   _____

5. In the art class, Dawn learns to identify several different figures. What is the name of the figure below?

   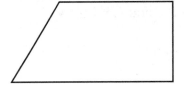

   _____

6. Dawn drew the following shape to represent her backyard. What is the name of the shape?

   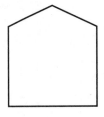

   _____

Lesson 10.1 Points and Lines

Read the problem carefully and solve. Show your work under each question.

April draws a design. She likes to label points and lines to help plan the design.

> **Helpful Hint**
>
> A line and a line segment use different symbols. A line continuously extends in two directions.

1. April included the following line in her design. How would you name the line, using geometric notation?

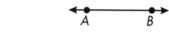

    _____ or _____

2. She plans to add line GH to her design. Draw the line GH below.

    _____

3. In the middle of the design, she decided to add the following line segment. How would she name this line segment?

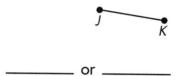

    _____ or _____

4. Next to line segment JK, April draws line segment WX into the design. Identify line segment WX using geometric notation.

    _____ or _____

5. April decides to change line segment WX to line WX. Identify line WX using geometric notation.

    _____ or _____

Lesson 10.2   Rays and Angles

Read the problem carefully and solve. Show your work under each question.

Alvin is helping to plan a playground for the neighborhood. The playground plan has many rays and angles.

Helpful Hint

An angle is the union of two rays. The middle of the angle is where the two rays meet.

1. One corner of the playground is represented using the angle shown below. Use geometric notation to name the angle in two ways.

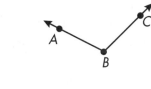

_____ or _____

2. Alvin draws a ray on the plan that shows the direction people will enter the playground. How would he label ray MN on the plans?

_____

3. Alvin combined two rays, $\overrightarrow{BA}$ and $\overrightarrow{BC}$, to make an angle at the edge of the playground plan. Draw and label this angle.

_____

4. Alvin was asked to draw angle RQS to represent the relationship of the slide to the ground. He drew the angle shown below. Did Alvin draw the angle correctly?

_____

5. The gate and the fence in the playground form the angle shown below. Name two geometric figures that are combined to make this angle?

_____

Lesson 10.3 Measuring Angles

Read the problem carefully and solve. Show your work under each question.

Alexis works in a mall. She notices all sorts of angles in the mall.

Helpful Hint

Use a protractor to measure an angle. Angles can be classified as **acute**, **obtuse**, or **right**. An acute angle measures less than 90°. An obtuse angle measures more than 90°. A right angle measures 90°.

1. A display in the mall contains the angle shown below. What type of angle is this?

_____

2. Alexis uses a protractor to find the actual measurement of the angle shown in question 1. What is the measure of the angle?

_____

3. The edge of the counter where Alexis works forms the angle shown below. Use a protractor to determine the measure of this angle. Then, classify the angle.

_____   _____

4. The angle below represents Alexis's walk from the mall entrance to the store where she works. Measure and classify the angle.

_____

5. Alexis told her mom that she can get to the mall office by walking straight from the entrance, then making an 85° turn and walking straight to get to the office. What kind of angle represents Alexis's route?

_____

Lesson 10.4 Vertical, Supplementary, and Complementary Angles

Read the problem carefully and solve. Show your work under each question.

Chang uses lines and angles to create a map of the streets near his home. The map is represented by the drawing to the right.

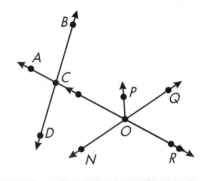

> **Helpful Hint**
>
> **Vertical** angles are opposite angles that have the same measure. **Supplementary** angles are two angles whose measures have a sum of 180°. **Complementary** angles are two angles whose measures have a sum of 90°. A **bisector** divides an angle into angles of equal measure.

1. Chang has a friend that lives at the corner represented by ∠BCO. Name the angle that is vertical to this angle.

   _____   _____

2. Chang notices that there appears to be two angle bisectors on the map. Which parts of the map appear to be a bisector?

   _____

3. Chang lives at the corner of ∠ACD. Name an angle that is supplementary to ∠ACD.

   _____ or _____

4. Chang's cousin lives along angle ∠DCA. What is the relationship of angle ∠DCA and ∠BCA?

   _____

5. Which angle must have the same measure as ∠ACB?

   _____

Lesson 10.5 Transversals

Read the problem carefully and solve. Show your work under each question.

Ivy likes to make pieces of art by putting together pieces of colored paper. Her father is helping her by cutting the pieces of colored paper. The figure to the right shows the initial plan for Ivy's art. In the figure, line *EF* is parallel to line *GH*.

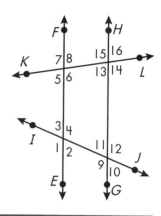

Helpful Hint

If the two lines being crossed are parallel, then:

- **Alternate interior angles** have the same measure.
- **Alternate exterior angles** have the same measure.
- **Corresponding angles** have the same measure.

3. Ivy tells her dad that she knows the measure of ∠5, and therefore knows three other angles that have the same measure. One is a vertical angle, one is a corresponding angle, and one is an alternate exterior angle. Which three angles does she mean?

_____ _____ _____

1. Ivy notices that some of the angle pairs for the design are equal. She identifies ∠15 and another angle as alternate interior angles. What is the other angle?

_____

4. Ivy names the angle that is an alternate interior angle with ∠2. Which angle does she name?

_____

2. Ivy tells her dad that ∠10 and ∠3 are equivalent. What term describes the relationship between these two angles?

_____

5. Ivy knows about angle relationships because she has studied transversals. Name the transversals in her plan.

_____

Lesson 10.6 Triangles (by angles) and Triangles (by side)

Read the problem carefully and solve. Show your work under each question.

Zeb is building a triangular sandbox for his younger sister. He isn't sure what type of triangle he wants to use for the shape of the sandbox, so he experiments by drawing plans with several different triangles.

Helpful Hint

Triangles can be named by their angles and side lengths. **Equilateral triangles** have three equal sides and 60° angles. **Isosceles triangles** have two equal sides and angles. **Scalene triangles** have no equal sides and angles.

1. Zeb draws a triangle for his sister, shown below. Based on its angles, what type of triangle is this?

_____

2. Zeb's sister draws a different triangle, shown below. Based on its sides, what type of triangle is this?

_____

3. Zeb tells his sister that they could use 3 pieces of wood they already have to make the edges of the sandbox. The 3 pieces of wood are all different lengths. Based on the lengths of the pieces, what type of triangle would these pieces of wood make?

_____

4. Zeb's sister likes the idea of having 2 of the sandbox edges the same length, so she drew the triangle shown below. Based on its side lengths and angles, name the type of triangle that Zeb's sister drew.

_____

5. After considering all the possibilities, Zeb and his sister decide that they will build an equilateral triangle for the sandbox. Describe the side lengths and angles of this triangle.

_____

Lesson 10.7 Quadrilaterals

Read the problem carefully and solve. Show your work under each question.

Erin is studying quadrilaterals. She learns that small changes in a quadrilateral can give it a new name. She practices the definitions of quadrilaterals by drawing figures on index cards and then writing the definitions on the back of the cards.

Helpful Hint

A **quadrilateral** is a closed figure with 4 sides. A **parallelogram** is a quadrilateral whose opposite sides are parallel and congruent. A **rectangle** is a parallelogram with four right angles. A **rhombus** is a parallelogram with four congruent sides. A **square** has four right angles and four congruent sides. A **trapezoid** is a quadrilateral with only one pair of parallel sides.

1. The definition on the back of one card reads, "a parallelogram with 4 congruent sides." Draw and label two different figures that fit this description.

2. Erin's sister asks her if all squares are also rectangles. How does Erin respond?

_____

_____

3. The shape below is on the front of one card. Which 2 terms will Erin use to name the shape?

_____ and _____

4. Erin sees the figure shown below on another card as she reviews for a quiz. What terms can be used to name this figure?

_____

5. Erin's sister asks if any square can also be called a rhombus. How should Erin answer the question?

_____

_____

Lesson 10.8 Polygons

Read the problem carefully and solve. Show your work under each question.

Jerry draws different polygons in the sand at the beach. He plays a game where he asks each family member to identify the polygons he draws.

> **Helpful Hint**
>
> A **polygon** is a closed figure whose sides are all line segments. Polygons can be classified by the number of sides they have. For example, a 5-sided polygon is called a **pentagon** and a 6-sided polygon is called a **hexagon**. Some other prefixes are: **hepta-** (7), **octa-** (8), **nona-** (9), and **deca-** (10).

1. Jerry draws a 10-sided figure. What is the name of the polygon?

   _____

3. Jerry drew a heptagon. Draw a heptagon below.

4. Jerry asks his mother to name the figure below that he drew in the sand. What is the name of the figure?

   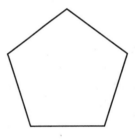

   _____

2. Jerry drew the figure below. What is the name of this figure?

   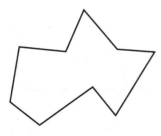

   _____

5. Jerry asks his father to name the figure below that he drew. How does his father respond?

   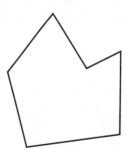

   _____

Lesson 10.9 Similar Figures

Read the problem carefully and solve. Show your work under each question.

Ella draws pairs of figures and writes the ratio of their sides in order to determine if the figures are similar.

Helpful Hint

Two figures are **similar** if their corresponding angles are congruent and the lengths of their corresponding sides are proportional. Write a ratio to determine if the sides are proportional.

1. Ella draws the figures below. What would the missing measure have to be for the triangles to be similar?

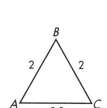
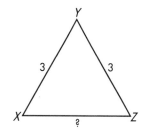

_____

2. Ella draws the figures below to model drawings for her new kitchen. How can you tell that the figures are not similar without calculating the ratios?

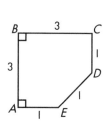
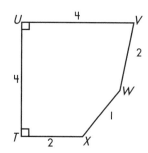

_____

3. Ella draws two pictures of kites below. Are the kites similar?

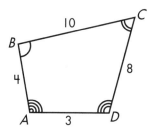
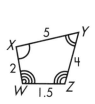

_____

4. Ella draws the figures below to model drawings for her patio. Using ratios of the side lengths, show if the figures are similar or not similar.

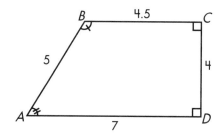
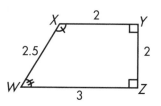

_____

Lesson 10.10 Plotting Ordered Pairs

Read the problem carefully and solve. Show your work under each question.

Irene draws a coordinate plane and plots points to help her decide where to paint flowers on her bedroom wall. The grid is shown to the right.

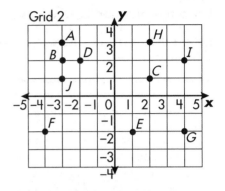

Grid 2

Helpful Hint

In a **coordinate plane**, the axes are labeled x and y. The coordinates of a point are represented by the ordered pair (x, y). The plane is divided into four quadrants. The x-value of the ordered pair tells you how to move along the horizontal axis and the y-value tells you how to move along the vertical axis.

1. Irene plans to paint a lilac flower at point (4, 2) on the grid. Which letter represents this point?

_____

2. If Irene moves point *H* two units to the right, what will be the coordinate location of the new point on the grid?

_____

3. Irene plans to paint a rose at point (−3, 3) on the grid. Which letter represents this point?

_____

4. Irene is trying to decide what type of flower to paint at point (−3, 2). She thinks that she will paint a lily at this point. Which letter represents point (−3, 2)?

_____

5. Irene plans to paint a daisy on the grid at a spot that is marked with the letter G. Which ordered pair represents point G?

_____

Lesson 10.11 Transformations

Read the problem carefully and solve. Show your work under each question.

Felipe uses transformations to make designs on T-shirts. He then paints the transformed shapes different colors.

Helpful Hint

A **transformation** is a change of the position or size of an image. In a **translation**, an image slides in any direction. In a **reflection**, an image is flipped over a line. In a **rotation**, an image is turned around on a point. In a **dilation**, an image is enlarged or reduced.

1. Felipe uses the transformation below to make his most popular T-shirt. What type of transformation is represented on the T-shirt?

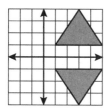

_____

2. One customer requested the figures below as the image on a T-shirt. What type of transformation do these shapes represent?

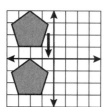

_____

3. The figure below was requested on a T-shirt by Felipe's neighbor. What type of transformation is represented on the T-shirt?

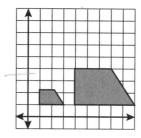

_____

4. The design shown below is the first image that Felipe ever put on a T-shirt. Which type of transformation is represented by this image?

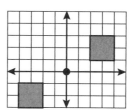

_____

5. Felipe is making a new design for T-shirts. The design is represented by the figure below. What type of transformation is shown?

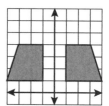

_____

Check What You Learned

Geometry

Read the problem carefully and solve. Show your work under each question.

Wyatt reviews figures that he has learned in class. He practices what he has learned by sketching shapes.

1. Wyatt draws the following triangle. Then, he asks his brother to name the triangle based on its sides and angles. How does he name the triangle?

_____

3. Wyatt draws the transformation shown below to practice indentifying transformations and points on a coordinate grid. What transformation does the drawing represent? What ordered pair is represented by point A'?

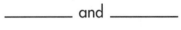 and _____

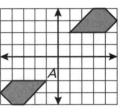

2. Wyatt draws the following two rectangles. Are the rectangles similar or not similar?

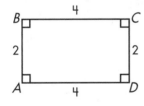

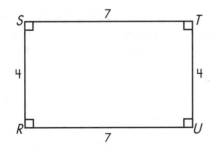

_____

4. Wyatt draws the angle shown below. He wants to draw an angle that is complementary to this angle. Draw an angle that is complementary to this angle.

_____

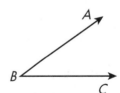

NAME _____

Check What You Know

Perimeter, Area, and Volume

Read the problem carefully and solve. Show your work under each question.

Greg spends a week over the summer at an overnight camp. He records many things about his environment while at camp.

1. The layout of the camp is represented by the drawing shown below. There is a fence around the property. How long is the fence?

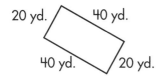

_____ yards

2. The camp has a pool that is in the shape of a circle, shown below. There is a tile trim around the edge of the pool. How long is the tile trim?

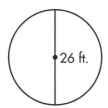

_____ feet

3. The pool has a depth of 5 feet. How much water can the pool hold?

_____ cubic feet

4. Greg makes a clay slate in one of his activities at camp. The picture below shows the slate. What is the area of the slate?

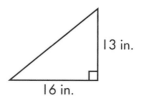

_____ square inches

5. The figure below is a wood storage box that Greg makes at camp. What is the volume of the box?

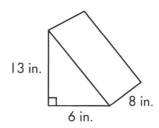

_____ cubic inches

6. Greg makes the following object while at camp and wants to paint its sides. What is the surface area of the object?

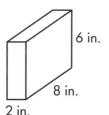

_____ square inches

Lesson 11.1 Perimeter

Read the problem carefully and solve. Show your work under each question.

Joanna works for a fencing company. Her job is to determine the amount of fencing needed for various clients.

> **Helpful Hint**
>
> The **perimeter** of a figure is the sum of the lengths of its sides. If two or more sides are equal, the formula can be simplified with multiplication.

1. Joanna needs to determine the perimeter of an animal pen. How many yards is the perimeter of the pen?

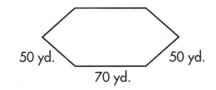

_____ yards

2. The figure below represents a city park in the shape of a regular pentagon. The city puts a fence around the park. How many yards of fencing is needed?

_____ yards

3. A parking lot is represented by the rectangle below. Joanna's company is hired to put a fence around the lot. How many yards of fencing will be needed?

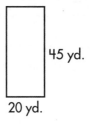

_____ yards

4. A dog park is in the shape of the square below. Joanna's company is going to put a fence around this park. How many meters of fencing will be needed?

18 m

_____ meters

5. The lot for a school is shown below. Joanna was called in to figure out how much fencing is needed. How many feet of fencing is needed to enclose the lot?

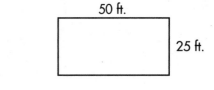

_____ feet

Lesson 11.2   Area of Rectangles

Read the problem carefully and solve. Show your work under each question.

Ivan sells rugs that are either square or rectangular in shape. He prices the rugs based on their square footage.

> **Helpful Hint**
>
> **Area** is the number of square units it takes to cover a figure. To find the area of a rectangle, multiply the length by the width.

1. Ivan sells the rug below to a new customer. What is the area of this rug?

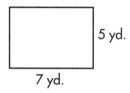

7 yd.

_____ square yards

2. The most popular rug that Ivan sells is represented by the figure below. A customer at the store wants to know the area of this rug. Write the area below.

12 ft.

10 ft.

_____ square feet

3. On Saturday, Ivan sells a large rug to a restaurant. The rug measures 24 feet by 18 feet. What is the area of the rug?

_____ square feet

4. Ivan sells the rug shown below with an area of 308 square feet. What is the width of this rug?

22 ft.

_____ feet

5. A hotel buys the square rug below for the lobby. What is the area of this rug?

5 m

_____ square meters

Lesson 11.3 Area of Triangles

Read the problem carefully and solve. Show your work under each question.

Hugo makes ceramic tiles that are triangular in shape. He sells his tiles to friends and businesses in the town where he lives.

Helpful Hint

The area of a triangle is the product of $\frac{1}{2}$ the base times the height.

1. One type of tile Hugo makes that is often purchased for kitchen counters is shown below. Find the area of the tile.

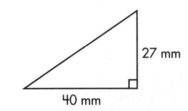

27 mm

40 mm

_____ square millimeters

2. Hugo makes tiles for his mother in the shape shown below. She plans to use them in her living room. What is the area of each tile?

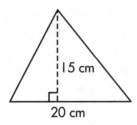

15 cm

20 cm

_____ square centimeters

3. Hugo makes a pattern using only tiles like the one shown below. He wants to know how many tiles can fit on the counter where he is building out the pattern. Find the area of each tile.

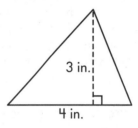

3 in.

4 in.

_____ square inches

4. Hugo makes the tile below for a storefront sign. The area of the tile is 552 square inches. What is the height?

46 in.

_____ inches

5. A set of tiles like the one below is made for a project. Hugo needs to find the area of each tile used. What is the area of each tile?

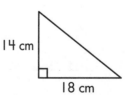

14 cm

18 cm

_____ square centimeters

Lesson 11.4 Circumference of Circles

Read the problem carefully and solve. Show your work under each question.

Essie works at a pizza shop. She helps with all aspects of the pizza shop. For the items below, use 3.14 for π.

> **Helpful Hint**
>
> A **circle** is a set of points that are all the same distance from a given point, called a **center**. The **perimeter** of a circle is called the **circumference**. The **diameter** is a segment that passes through the center of the circle and has both endpoints on the circle. The **radius** is a segment that has as its endpoints the circle and the center.

1. The main circular dining section in the pizza shop has a diameter of 40 feet. What is the circumference of the dining section?

   _____ feet

2. Each table was protected with a plastic strip around the outside edge. Each table has a diameter of 3 feet. What is the length of each plastic strip?

   _____ feet

3. An individual-sized pizza has a radius of 4 inches. What is the circumference?

   _____ inches

4. Essie puts a rim of cheese around the edge of the medium-sized pizza. The length of the cheese rim is 37.68 inches long. Find the radius of the pizza.

   _____ inches

5. The pizza shop sells a large pizza that has an 8-inch radius. Essie needs to know the circumference of the large pizza to order the correct sized boxes for delivery. What is the circumference of this pizza?

   _____ inches

Lesson 11.5 Area of Circles

Read the problem carefully and solve. Show your work under each question.

Javon works for a company that makes kitchenware. Javon is in charge of determining the amount of materials they will need to make circular plates, vases, and platters.

> **Helpful Hint**
>
> The *area* of a circle is found by using the formula $A = \pi r^2$. Remember, π can be expressed as 3.14.

1. The circle below represents one of the plates the company makes. What is the area of this plate?

_____ square inches

2. The bottom of a vase is in the shape of a circle. Javon measures the diameter of the bottom and it is 18 cm. What is the area of the bottom of the vase?

_____ square centimeters

3. A large ceramic wheel that the company sells is shown below. What is the area of the wheel?

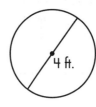

_____ square feet

4. A platter made at Javon's company is in the shape of a circle with a radius of 8 inches. What is the area of the platter?

_____ square inches

5. Javon packages plates that are 24 cm in diameter. He wants to know the area of each plate. What is the area of each plate?

_____ square centimeters

Lesson 11.6 Area of Irregular Shapes

Read the problem carefully and solve. Show your work under each question.

Olivia learns about irregular shapes in school. Then, she begins to notice all sorts of irregular shapes in the world around her.

Helpful Hint

To find the area of irregular shapes, separate the shapes into figures for which you can find the area, like triangles, squares, and rectangles. Then, add those areas together.

1. Olivia looks at a drawing of her parents' property and then draws the shape below to represent it. What is the area of the property?

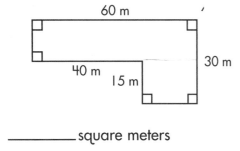

_____ square meters

2. Olivia's family has a cottage by a lake. The picture below shows the layout of the cottage. What is the area?

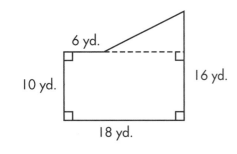

_____ square yards

3. Olivia finds a plastic shape in her house that has the dimensions shown below. What is the area of the shape?

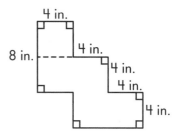

_____ square inches

4. To help her father order paint for the front of the house, Olivia calculates the area using the drawing shown below. What is the area?

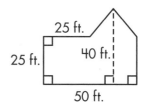

_____ square feet

5. Olivia makes a card to give to her father for Father's Day. The shape of the card is shown below. The area of the card is 75 square inches. What is the height?

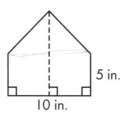

_____ inches

Lesson 11.7   Surface Area (Rectangular Solids)

Read the problem carefully and solve. Show your work under each question.

Mr. Benson sells packaging boxes. The boxes come in a variety of sizes.

> **Helpful Hint**
>
> The **surface area** of a solid is the sum of the areas of all the faces (or surfaces of the solid). The surface area of a rectangular solid can be found by the formula
> $SA = 2lw + 2lh + 2wh$.

1. The most popular-sized box Mr. Benson sells has the dimensions of 32 cm by 12 cm by 26 cm. What is the surface area of this box?

_____ square centimeters

2. Mr. Benson has a customer who wants to know the surface area of the box below so she can buy enough gift-wrap for the box. What is the surface area of the box?

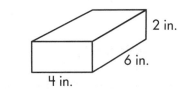

_____ square inches

3. One of Mr. Benson's customers buys the box below to send some books through the mail. What is the surface area of the box?

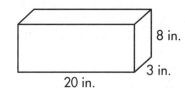

_____ square inches

4. The picture below represents the building that Mr. Benson works in. The surface area of the building is 416 square yards. What is the height of the building?

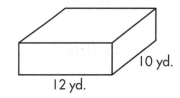

_____ yards

5. Mr. Benson buys a jewelry box for his daughter. The box measures 7 inches by 5 inches by 3 inches. What is the surface area of the box?

_____ square inches

Lesson 11.8 Volume of Rectangular Solids

Read the problem carefully and solve. Show your work under each question.

Daysha works on a container ship that carries cargo. Daysha records the volume of each container that is loaded onto the ship.

Helpful Hint

The **volume** of a rectangular solid is the product of the length times the width times the height. The formula for the volume is $V = lwh$. Volume is expressed in cubic units.

1. One of the containers on the ship contains cameras. The dimensions of this container are shown below. Find the volume of the container.

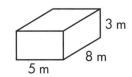

_____ cubic meters

2. The container shown below is filled with office supplies and loaded onto the ship by Daysha. The volume of the container is 225 cubic feet. What is the width?

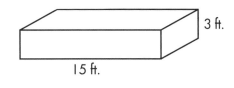

_____ feet

3. Daysha loads a container onto the ship that is packed with furniture. The drawing below shows the dimensions of this container. What is its volume?

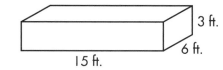

_____ cubic feet

4. One of the heavier containers Daysha loads onto the ship is shown below. What is the volume of this container?

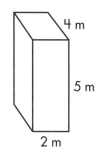

_____ cubic meters

5. One of the containers Daysha loads onto the ship is shown below. The volume of the container is 1,200 cubic feet. What is the length of the container?

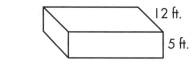

_____ feet

Lesson 11.9 Volume of Triangular Solids

Read the problem carefully and solve. Show your work under each question.

Ashton makes models and doorstops using blocks of wood. When he is planning what to make, he calculates the volume of each piece so he knows how much wood to purchase.

Helpful Hint

The bases of a triangular solid are triangles. To find the volume, multiply the area of one base times the height.

1. The first piece of wood that Ashton uses in his model is the block shown below. What is the volume of the block?

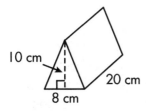

_____ cubic centimeters

2. The second block Ashton makes for the model is shown below. What is the volume of this block?

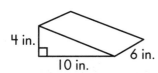

_____ cubic inches

3. The piece of wood shown below will be used as a decorative doorstop. What is its volume?

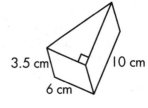

_____ cubic centimeters

4. Ashton packs his blocks onto a container shown below. What is the volume of the container?

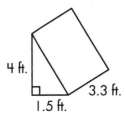

_____ cubic feet

5. Ashton adds the final block, shown below, to his model. What is the volume of this block?

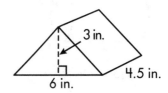

_____ cubic inches

Lesson 11.10 Surface Area (Cylinders)

Read the problem carefully and solve. Show your work under each question.

Cheryl has just learned about cylinders in geometry. She collects all the cylinders she can find to practice finding the surface area of a cylinder. Use 3.14 for π.

Helpful Hint

A **cylinder** can be represented on a flat surface as two circles for the bases and a rectangle. The height of the cylinder is the width of the rectangle. The circumference of the base is the length. The surface area is the sum of the area of these three surfaces. It is found by the formula: $2\pi r^2 + 2\pi rh$.

1. Cheryl finds that she has a cooler for ice in the shape of a cylinder. A diagram of the cooler is shown below. What is the surface area of the cooler?

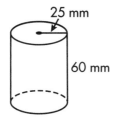

25 mm

60 mm

_____ square millimeters

2. An old container, shown below, was used to ship a rug to Cheryl's house. What is the surface area of the container?

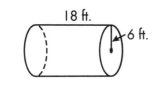

18 ft.

6 ft.

_____ square feet

3. A container used to store sea salt is shown below. The surface area of the container is 439.6 square inches. What is the height?

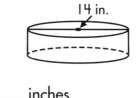

14 in.

_____ inches

4. Cheryl has a container where she stores old blankets and bedding. A picture of the container is shown below. What is the surface area of the cylinder?

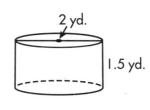

2 yd.

1.5 yd.

_____ square yards

5. There is a hatbox in Cheryl's garage like the one shown below. What is the surface area of the box?

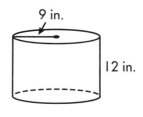

9 in.

12 in.

_____ square inches

Lesson 11.11 Volume of Cylinders

Read the problem carefully and solve. Show your work under each question.

Bill has a set of plastic storage containers. He calculates the volume of each container.

> **Helpful Hint**
>
> The volume of a cylinder is the product of the area of the base (*B*) times the height. The formula for the volume of a cylinder is:
> $V = Bh$

1. Bill has one container below in which he will store rice. How much rice will the container hold?

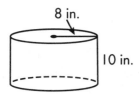

8 in.

10 in.

_____ cubic inches

2. Bill usually stores homemade salad dressing in the container below. How many cubic centimeters of dressing can the container hold?

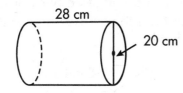

28 cm

20 cm

_____ cubic centimeters

3. The container below is used by Bill to store dried herbs. Find the volume of the container.

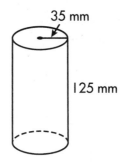

35 mm

125 mm

_____ cubic millimeters

4. The container below can hold 530.66 cubic inches of coffee. What is its height?

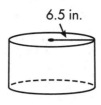

6.5 in.

_____ inches

5. Bill uses the container shown below to store pasta. How much pasta can the container hold?

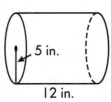

5 in.

12 in.

_____ cubic inches

Check What You Learned

Perimeter, Area, and Volume

Read the problem carefully and solve. Show your work under each question.

Delia works in the maintenance department for a local business.

1. Delia has an office space, shown below, that is in the shape of a square. She needs to run an electric cord around the edge of the space. How long will the cord be?

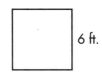

6 ft.

_____ feet

2. On her wall, Delia has a small clock, shown below. What is the circumference of the clock?

14 cm

_____ centimeters

3. The diagram below represents Delia's office building. The maintenance crew needs to calculate the total volume of the building for the new air-conditioning system. What is the volume of the building?

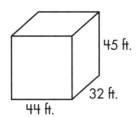

45 ft.
32 ft.
44 ft.

_____ cubic feet

4. The company that Delia works for has a lunchroom. The picture below shows the room. What is its area?

20 ft.
16 ft.

_____ square feet

5. Delia has a novelty coffee mug that is in the shape shown below. What is the volume of this mug?

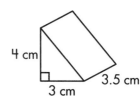

4 cm
3.5 cm
3 cm

_____ cubic centimeters

6. Delia has a bin to store her paper clips in. What are the surface area and volume of the bin?

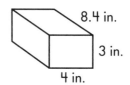

8.4 in.
3 in.
4 in.

_____ square inches

_____ cubic inches

Check What You Know

Variables, Expressions, and Equations

Read the problem carefully and solve. Show your work under each question.

Dylan likes to work with numbers. He likes to make everyday situations into puzzles that he can then solve. The problems below show some examples of how he does this.

---

1. Dylan has two books by the same author. Book A was published five years earlier than the other book. If book A is represented by the letter *x*, what statement can Dylan write to represent the age of the other book?

_____

2. Dylan ordered a box of pencils. The box contains *y* pencils. Dylan divides the pencils evenly among 4 friends. What expression does Dylan write to find how many pencils each friend gets?

_____

3. Dylan adds a number, *n*, to 8 and gets a total of 26. What equation could Dylan write to represent this situation?

_____

4. Dylan buys 3 orange drinks on Tuesday and 5 orange drinks on Wednesday. The drinks cost $2 each. Write an equation using the Distributive Property to represent this situation.

_____

5. Dylan plays a game with cards. The following expression shows how many points he got. How many points did Dylan get?

$$-5 + (-3) \div (2 - 1)$$

_____

6. In one of Dylan's puzzles, he has the expression 2^{-2}. How is this written as a fraction?

_____

Lesson 12.1 Variables, Expressions, and Equations

Read the problem carefully and solve. Show your work under each question.

Drew has a class project that makes him look into his family history. Within the project, he compares the ages of many of his family members. He uses variables, expressions, and equations to represent the ages of his family members in his project.

Helpful Hint

An **expression** is a way of naming a number. A **numerical expression** contains only numbers. A **variable expression** contains numbers and variables. An **equation** is a mathematical sentence that states that two expressions are equal. An **inequality** is a mathematical sentence that states that two expressions are not equal.

1. Drew starts his project with his immediate family members. Drew is 4 years older than his sister, Carol. If Carol is represented by the letter c, what expression represents Drew's age in relation to his sister's age?

_____

2. Drew's father is 5 years younger than his mother. If m represents his mother's age, what expression represents Drew's father's age?

_____

3. Drew's grandmother is 72 years old. Drew's mother is y years younger than Drew's grandmother, and she is 45 years old. Write an equation using subtraction that represents this situation.

_____

4. Drew is three times the age of his cousin, Steve. Write an equation to represent this relationship. Use division, d for Drew, and s for Steve.

_____

5. Drew's sister Carol is more than twice the age of their youngest sibling, Abe. Write an inequality to represent this situation using c for Carol's age and a for Abe's age.

_____

Lesson 12.2 Number Properties

Read the problem carefully and solve. Show your work under each question.

Zaina and Hunter often work on their homework together. They are writing problems for each other where they have to name the property used in the problem.

Helpful Hint

Associative property:
$a + (b + c) = (a + b) + c$

Commutative property: $a + b = b + a$

Identity property: $a \times 1 = a$ and $a + 0 = a$

Multiplication property of zero: $a \times 0 = 0$

1. Zaina writes the following equation and Hunter is asked to identify the number property. What is Hunter's answer?

   $25 + p = p + 25$

   _____

2. Hunter asks Zaina to write a difficult equation. Zaina writes the equation below. Hunter says he can solve it immediately without making any calculations. Which number property did Hunter use?

   $41 \times 115 \times 0 \times 52 \times 1{,}273 = ?$

   _____

3. Hunter says that the expression $4 \times (t \times 5)$ has the same value as $(4 \times t) \times 5$. Which number property helps Hunter make this statement?

   _____

4. Zaina says: "Adding zero to any number does not change its value." Which property is represented by Zaina's statement?

   _____

5. Hunter writes the following equation. Which number property is represented by this equation?

   $9{,}456{,}845 \times 1 = 9{,}456{,}845$

   _____

Lesson 12.3 The Distributive Property

Read the problem carefully and solve. Show your work under each question.

Irene studies the distributive property and finds ways to use it in her everyday life. The situations shown below demonstrate this concept.

Helpful Hint

The **distributive property** combines multiplication with addition or subtraction. The property states:
$a \times (b + c) = (a \times b) + (a \times c)$
$a \times (b - c) = (a \times b) - (a \times c)$

---

1. Irene rents a canoe for 2 hours in the morning and for 3 more hours in the afternoon. The rental company charges $15 per hour for the rental. Write an expression using the distributive property to represent this situation.

   _____

2. Irene orders 4 boxes of notepads one week and 7 boxes of notepads the next week. Each box costs a dollars. She writes the following expression: $(a \times 4) + (a \times 7)$

   Rewrite the expression using the distributive property.

   _____

3. Irene buys 5 pairs of shirts. The shirts cost $22 each. Use the distributive property to write an expression that will make it easier for Irene to determine the total cost of the shirts.

   _____

4. Irene and four friends each had coupons for $2 off admission to a water park. If admission is $11, write an expression using the distributive property to represent the total cost of admission for all 5 people.

   _____

5. Irene has to paint 8 mugs. It takes v minutes to paint a mug and m minutes to dry. Write an equation relating two expressions that will help Irene calculate the total amount of time it will take to finish the mugs. Use the distributive property.

   _____

Lesson 12.4 Order of Operations

Read the problem carefully and solve. Show your work under each question.

Ahmed likes to represent everyday situations in his life using expressions.

Helpful Hint

Order of operations

1. All operations within parentheses

2. All exponents

3. All multiplication and division, from left to right

4. All addition and subtraction, from left to right

1. Ahmed buys cans of seltzer water in packs of six cans. One day, he buys 4 packs of six cans and then another 3 individual cans of seltzer. He uses the expression below to represent the purchase. How many cans in total did he buy?

   $3 + 4 \times 4$

   _____

2. Ahmed writes the expression below to show how players were divided into teams for a game and how extra players were added. What is the value of the expression?

   $18 \div (2 + 1) + 2$

   _____

3. Ahmed played a game using the expression below. If he answered correctly, he gets to write the next expression. What is the value of the expression?

   $42 \div 6 + 8$

   _____

4. Ahmed tosses 5 pennies into a wishing well. He then tosses 2 more pennies in the pool. He did this 2 days in a row. Use the expression below to find the total number of pennies Ahmed tossed into the well.

   $2 \times (2 + 5)$

   _____

5. Ahmed writes the expression below to represent the number of games he has acquired or lost over the past few years. How many games does he have?

   $(8 - 4) \times (4 + 2) + 2$

   _____

Lesson 12.5 Solving Addition and Subtraction Equations

Read the problem carefully and solve. Show your work under each question.

Lin sells cars for a living. She keeps track of her sales data each week.

Helpful Hint

Subtraction Property of Equality: When two expressions are equal, if you subtract the same number from both expressions, the difference will also be equal.

Addition Property of Equality: When two expressions are equal, if you add the same number to both expressions, the sums will also be equal.

1. Lin sells 7 more cars this week than she did in week a. She sold 16 cars this week. How many cars did she sell in week a?

$7 + a = 16$

_____

2. Lin writes the following equation to represent the total number of cars she expects to sell this week, b, minus the number of cars she has already sold. How many cars does she expect to sell?

$b - 17 = 3$

_____

3. Lin writes the following equation to represent the number of cars she sells in one day, d, plus another day. How many cars does she sell on day d?

$9 = d + 4$

_____

4. Lin writes the following equation to represent the selling price of a car minus the cost for the dealership to get the car. What was the cost, c, of the car?

$\$4{,}000 - c = \$350$

_____

5. Lin writes the following equation to represent the number of cars she needs to sell in week g. How many cars does she need to sell in week g?

$15 = g + 12$

_____

Lesson 12.6 Solving Multiplication and Division Equations

Read the problem carefully and solve. Show your work under each question.

Mrs. Ross orders supplies for her classroom and then distributes them to the students in her classroom.

Helpful Hint

Division Property of Equality: When two expressions are equal, if they are divided by the same number, the quotients will also be equal.

Multiplication Property of Equality: When two expressions are equal, if they are multiplied by the same number, the products will also be equal.

1. Mrs. Ross orders pencils that come in packs of 16. The equation below represents the pencils she ordered. How many packs did she order?

$n \times 16 = 32$

_____

2. Mrs. Ross orders notepads that come in packs of 4. The equation below represents the notepads she ordered. How many notepads did she order in total?

$m \times 4 = 24$

_____

3. Mrs. Ross orders binders. She divides them evenly among the 24 students. Each student gets 3 binders. Use the equation below to find the total number of binders.

$a \div 24 = 3$

_____

4. Mrs. Ross orders highlighters for her students. She divides them evenly among the students. Each student gets 6 highlighters. Use the equation below to find the number of students.

$144 \div s = 6$

_____

5. Mrs. Ross orders pens that come in packs of 12. The equation below represents the pens she ordered. How many pens did she order in total?

$z \times 12 = 48$

_____

Lesson 12.7 Adding, Subtracting, Multiplying, and Dividing Integers

Read the problem carefully and solve. Show your work under each question.

Owen is the manager for the high school football team. He keeps track of team statistics.

Helpful Hint

The sum of two positive integers is positive. The sum of two negative integers is negative. The product or quotient of two integers with the same sign is positive. The product or quotient of two integers with different signs is negative.

1. Owen writes the expression below to represent the yards gained in the last three plays of a game. Find the sum.

   $14 + (-7) + (-3)$

   _____

2. The expression below is used by Owen to find the difference in yards gained by two different players. What is the difference?

   $15 - (-10)$

   _____

3. Each time the team loses, they lose 7 points in the standings. Use the expression below to show the total number of points lost from their 5 losses.

   $5 \times (-7)$

   _____

4. Owen writes the expression below to represent the average yards lost in the teams worst 8 plays last week. What was the average loss per play?

   $-32 \div 8$

   _____

5. Owen uses the expression below when calculating one of the team's statistics at the end of the year. What is the product?

   $-7 \times (-3)$

   _____

Lesson 12.8 Multiplying and Dividing Powers

Read the problem carefully and solve. Show your work under each question.

Yuri keeps track of various data in New Evansville. He uses exponents to represent large numbers.

Helpful Hint

A **power** is a number that is expressed using an **exponent**. The **base** is the number that is multiplied, and the exponent tells how many times the base is used as a factor.

1. Yuri writes the expression 6^3 to represent the number of seventh-grade students in the school district. How many seventh-grade students are in the district?

   _____ students

2. Yuri uses the expression 4^4 to represent the number of clients for an accounting firm in town. How many clients does the firm have?

   _____

3. The expression $5^2 \times 5^3$ represents the number of buildings times the number of occupants in the local college dormitories. What is the simplified form of this expression using one exponent?

   _____

4. There are 64 stoplights in town. How can this number be written using an exponent with a base of 2?

   _____

5. Yuri wants to rewrite 2^6 as the product of two expressions, both with exponents using 2 as the base. What does Yuri write?

   _____ $\times$ _____

Lesson 12.9 Negative Exponents

Read the problem carefully and solve. Show your work under each question.

Denise uses negative exponents to represent fractions. Some of her examples are shown below.

Helpful Hint

When a power includes a negative exponent, express the number as 1 divided by the base and change the exponent to positive. To multiply or divide powers with the same base, combine bases, add or subtract the exponents, then simplify.

1. Denise writes the expression 2^{-3}. How would you write this expression with a positive exponent?

_____

2. Denise writes the expression 8^{-2}. How would you write this expression with a positive exponent?

_____

3. Denise writes the expression 5^{-3}. How would you write this expression as a fraction with no exponent?

_____

4. Denise writes the expression $3^{-3} \times 3^{-3}$. What is the product?

_____

5. Denise writes the expression $6^{-4} \div 6^{-2}$. What is the product?

_____

Check What You Learned

Variables, Expressions, and Equations

Read the problem carefully and solve. Show your work under each question.

Hector writes variables, expressions, and equations to help him study for a test.

1. Hector brings *x* pairs of shorts on a 5-day vacation. He plans to wear 2 pairs per day. How many pairs of shorts did Hector bring on vacation?

_____ pairs of shorts

2. Hector runs a total of 12 miles. If he runs *c* miles each hour, write an expression to show the number of miles he runs each hour.

_____

3. Hector has 2^3 cans of peanuts, and each can contains 2^8 peanuts. How many peanuts does Hector have in all? Write your answer as a number with one exponent.

_____ peanuts

4. Hector has 48 paperclips, and he gives *h* paper clips to a friend. If he is left with 32 paperclips, write an equation that shows this situation.

_____

5. Hector gains 9 points in a game. Then in the next round, he loses 12 points. He writes the expression below to show this. How many points does he have in total?

$9 + (-12) =$ _____

6. Hector needs to work on dividing exponents. What is $3^{-3} \div 3^{-2}$?

_____

Final Test Chapters 1–12

Read the problem carefully and solve. Show your work under each question.

Evan is attending a picnic. Among the things he packs are 4 quarts of lemonade, a 34-inch loaf of french bread, and 57 ounces of potato salad.

1. Each quart of lemonade costs $4.29. How much money does Evan spend on lemonade for the picnic?

   _____

4. How many pounds of potato salad does Evan bring to the picnic?

   _____ pounds

2. Another person brings 3 quarts of lemonade. How many gallons of lemonade are there in all?

   _____ gallons

5. The cost of the potato salad is $27.96. If 12 people each eat the same amount of potato salad and there is none left over, how much is the cost per person?

   _____

3. How many feet of bread does Evan bring to the picnic? Show your answer as a mixed numeral.

   _____ feet

6. The picnic lasted 126 minutes. How many hours is this?

   _____ hours

Final Test Chapters 1–12

Read the problem carefully and solve. Show your work under each question.

Daysha buys a business making smoothies. She has chosen to purchase a smoothie machine because it is light enough to transport. The weight of the machine is 4.2 kilograms. The machine can hold up to 5 liters of liquid.

1. Daysha wants to know how many metric tons the machine weighs. Write the weight of the machine in metric tons.

_____ metric tons

2. Daysha makes a batch of smoothies and fills the machine $\frac{6}{20}$ full with strawberries. What percent of the smoothie machine is full?

_____

3. What is the total number of milliliters that the smoothie machine can hold?

_____ milliliters

4. The smoothie machine cord measures 58 centimeters in length. How many millimeters long is the cord?

_____ millimeters

5. Daysha writes the simple interest rate from her account, 3%, as a decimal. How do you write 3% as a decimal?

_____

6. Daysha deposits $500 she made over the weekend in her bank account. The account earns 3% simple interest. How much will the $500 yield after 5 years?

_____

Final Test Chapters 1–12

Read the problem carefully and solve. Show your work under each question.

India is surveying people from her booth at the mall. One survey asks 20 people their favorite color of car. The results are shown in the circle graph to the right.

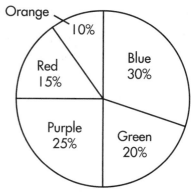

Favorite Color of Car

1. How many people said that green or red was their favorite color?

   _____ people

2. India surveys 20 people to find the number of hours each week that they exercise. The results in hours are: 2, 0, 4, 7, 1, 4, 3, 1, 3, 9, 1, 5, 3, 5, 2, 1, 3, 4, 2, 1. Make a line plot to show these results.

3. In her booth, India has a jar with different flavors of tea bags. The jar contains 12 tea bags, and 3 of them are green tea. Write the percentage of the tea bags that are green tea as a decimal and as a fraction.

   _____ and _____

4. The figure below is a drawing from one of India's surveys about car hood ornaments. Determine if the two shapes are similar, and what type of transformation was used to make the larger figure.

   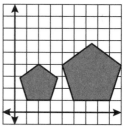

   _____ and _____

5. India uses the circle below to represent the clock in her booth. She wants to buy a decorative frame and a piece of glass to cover it. What is the circumference and area of the clock? Use 3.14 for π.

   _____ inches

   _____ square inches

Final Test Chapters 1–12

Read the problem carefully and solve. Show your work under each question.

Mrs. Jung created the box-and-whisker plot to the right to represent the class scores on a recent history test.

Test Scores on History Test

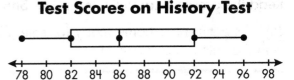

1. What is the median score of the history test?

   _____

2. The actual scores for the test are: 86, 92, 83, 79, 80, 81, 92, 83, 84, 87, 89, 92, 94, 78, 95, 96, and 85. What is the mean test score, rounded to the nearest whole number?

   _____

3. Mrs. Jung makes a stem-and-leaf plot using the list of actual scores from the test. Make a stem-and-leaf plot.

   _____

4. Mrs. Jung tells her students the range of the data for the test scores. What is the range?

   _____

5. To help decide who gets form A of the test, Mrs. Jung rolls a 12-sided number cube. It is numbered on each side with a number from 1–12. What is the probability that she will roll either a 2 or a 5? Write your answer as a percent rounded to the nearest whole percent.

   _____

6. Mrs. Jung has a container, shown below, to hold pencils and erasers. She wants to cover it with decorative fabric. What is the surface area and the volume of the container?

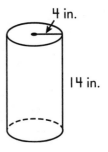

4 in.

14 in.

   _____ square inches

   _____ cubic inches

Final Test Chapters 1–12

Read the problem carefully and solve. Show your work under each question.

Jayla is getting her home ready for sale. She drew a floorplan and sketches of her house to include with the sale announcement.

1. Jayla draws the angle shown below to represent the angle of a wall in her closet. How would you name the angle using a symbol and letters?

_____ or _____

2. Jayla draws the triangle below to represent a window in her house. How would you name the triangle based on its sides and angles?

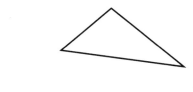

_____

Use the drawing below of Jayla's garden layout for numbers 3–5.

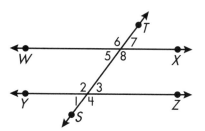

3. Which angle is vertical to ∠7?

∠ _____

4. Which angle along with ∠2 makes a pair of alternate interior angles?

∠ _____

5. Jayla wants to know which angle is a corresponding angle to ∠1. Which angle corresponds to ∠1?

∠ _____

6. Jayla buys p paint cans at $18.22 each. She spends a total of $91.10. Jayla writes the equation below to represent the situation. How many cans of paint does she buy?

$$\$18.22 \times p = \$91.10$$

_____ cans of paint

Final Test Chapters 1–12

Read the problem carefully and solve. Show your work under each question.

Grace works in a bank. The dimensions of the bank are shown on the right.

32 ft.

12 ft.

---

1. Grace calculates the perimeter and area of the bank building. What is the perimeter? What is the area?

   _____ feet _____ square feet

4. The following expression represents the calculations Grace made with a savings account. What is the value of the expression?
   $2 + 4 \times 4 - 5$

   _____

2. The expression below represents 2 deposits of $17 and 2 deposits of $85 into Grace's savings account. Use the distributive property to rewrite the expression.

   $2(\$17) + 2(\$85)$

   _____

5. Grace has a box on her desk where she keeps her personal belongings. The box measures 6 inches by 14 inches by 5 inches. What is the volume of the box?

   _____ cubic inches

3. Grace writes the following equation to represent the amount of money that she has in her bank account after buying groceries that total $45. How much money did she start with in her account?
   $x - \$45 = \$378$

   _____

6. Grace used the following expression to help combine rates for two different accounts. What is the simplified form of this expression with no exponents?

   $5^2 \times 5^{-3}$

   _____

Scoring Record for Posttests, Mid-Test, and Final Test

Chapter Posttest	Your Score	Performance			
		Excellent	Very Good	Fair	Needs Improvement
1	____ of 6	6	5	3–4	2 or fewer
2	____ of 6	6	5	3–4	2 or fewer
3	____ of 6	6	5	3–4	2 or fewer
4	____ of 6	6	5	3–4	2 or fewer
5	____ of 6	6	5	3–4	2 or fewer
6	____ of 6	6	5	3–4	2 or fewer
7	____ of 6	6	5	3–4	2 or fewer
8	____ of 6	6	5	3–4	2 or fewer
9	____ of 12	11–12	9–10	7–8	6 or fewer
10	____ of 4	4	3	2	1 or fewer
11	____ of 12	11–12	9–10	7–8	6 or fewer
12	____ of 6	6	5	3–4	2 or fewer
Mid-Test	____ of 24	22–24	20–21	16–19	15 or fewer
Final Test	____ of 35	33–35	29–32	23–28	22 or fewer

Record your test score in the Your Score column. See where your score falls in the Performance columns. Your score is based on the total number of required responses. If your score is fair or needs improvement, review the chapter material.

Grade 7 Answers

Chapter 1

Pretest, page 1
1. 24,368
2. 399,028
3. 40,620
4. 2,707
5. 2,031
6. 42,561

Lesson 1.1, page 2
1. 201,587
2. 56,647
3. 334,361
4. 132,774
5. 41,523

Lesson 1.2, page 3
1. 1,472
2. 63,612
3. 23,718
4. 39,648
5. 147,250

Lesson 1.3, page 4
1. 615; 2
2. 65
3. 732
4. 61; 22
5. 1,464

Posttest, page 5
1. 122,800
2. 8,174
3. 194,814
4. 27,174
5. 1,130
6. 4,529

Chapter 2

Pretest, page 6
1. 12
2. $\frac{8}{12} < \frac{9}{12}$, $\frac{3}{4}$
3. $1\frac{5}{12}$
4. $4\frac{3}{4}$
5. $86\frac{5}{8}$
6. $\frac{5}{12}$

Lesson 2.1, page 7
1. 16
2. 9
3. 6
4. 4
5. 12

Lesson 2.2, page 8
1. $\frac{11}{30}$
2. $\frac{2}{15}$
3. The probability of the event occurring is a fraction between 0 and 1.
4. $\frac{4}{15}$
5. $\frac{1}{12}$

Lesson 2.3, page 9
1. Marlene: $\frac{10}{12}$, Bianca: $\frac{5}{12}$
2. Kareem
3. $\frac{20}{24} > \frac{15}{24}$
4. 48
5. Paul

Lesson 2.4, page 10
1. $3\frac{4}{7}$
2. $3\frac{3}{4}$
3. $\frac{37}{8}$
4. $\frac{20}{9}$
5. $\frac{33}{5}$

Lesson 2.5, page 11
1. $1\frac{27}{56}$
2. $\frac{1}{8}$
3. $1\frac{4}{15}$
4. $3\frac{9}{35}$
5. $\frac{5}{12}$

Lesson 2.6, page 12
1. $3\frac{3}{8}$
2. 4
3. $7\frac{1}{3}$
4. $\frac{1}{4}$
5. $\frac{2}{9}$

Lesson 2.7, page 13
1. $\frac{19}{15}$
2. $\frac{1}{45}$
3. $\frac{7}{33}$
4. $\frac{9}{4}$
5. $\frac{9}{29}$

Lesson 2.8, page 14
1. $2\frac{2}{7}$
2. $1\frac{5}{6}$
3. $8\frac{2}{3}$
4. $\frac{7}{8}$
5. $1\frac{1}{4}$

Grade 7 Answers

Posttest, page 15
1. 10
2. $\frac{7}{10} < \frac{4}{5}$
3. $1\frac{1}{2}$
4. $1\frac{1}{8}$
5. $153\frac{1}{32}$
6. $3\frac{1}{12}$

Chapter 3

Pretest, page 16
1. $4,318.35
2. 3.375
3. $4,318.35
4. $676.38
5. 13
6. $1,947.60

Lesson 3.1, page 17
1. 0.125
2. 1.75
3. 0.285
4. $\frac{7}{50}$
5. $3\frac{3}{8}$

Lesson 3.2, page 18
1. 32.548
2. 13.315
3. 14.03
4. 21.435
5. 38.748

Lesson 3.3, page 19
1. 19.27
2. 18.14
3. 8.575
4. 21.06
5. 2.92

Lesson 3.4, page 20
1. 14.175
2. 18.275
3. 47.5
4. 1.875
5. 24.65

Lesson 3.5, page 21
1. $14.15
2. $32.99
3. $1.98
4. $26.78
5. 1.1784

Lesson 3.6, page 22
1. 40
2. 48
3. 60
4. 170
5. 1.1342

Lesson 3.7, page 23
1. 30
2. 42
3. 17
4. 30
5. 264.12; 264

Posttest, page 24
1. $2,755.08
2. $12.35
3. $694.30
4. $533.28
5. 12
6. $2\frac{14}{25}$

Chapter 4

Pretest, page 25
1. 0.25
2. $1\frac{3}{4} > 1.7$
3. $\frac{3}{10}$
4. $\frac{1}{3}$, 34%, 0.35
5. 12%
6. 6

Lesson 4.1, page 26
1. $\frac{39}{50}$; 0.78
2. $\frac{4}{5}$; 0.8
3. $\frac{13}{20}$; 0.65
4. $\frac{47}{50}$; 0.94
5. $\frac{22}{25}$; 0.88

Lesson 4.2, page 27
1. $40\% > \frac{1}{4}$
2. $3.68 < 3\frac{4}{5}$
3. $\frac{1}{4} > 0.15$
4. 40%, 3.68, $3\frac{4}{5}$
5. 105%, $\frac{11}{10}$, 1.111, $1\frac{1}{4}$

Lesson 4.3, page 28
1. $\frac{2}{25}$
2. 35%
3. $\frac{11}{50}$
4. 50%
5. $1\frac{1}{4}$

Lesson 4.4, page 29
1. 0.12
2. 58%
3. 6%
4. 0.02
5. 0.62

Lesson 4.5, page 30
1. 9
2. 12

Grade 7 Answers

3. 6
4. 18
5. 51

Posttest, page 31
1. 0.14
2. $0.62 < \frac{5}{8}$
3. $1\frac{7}{20}$
4. 4%, 0.44, $\frac{3}{4}$
5. $13\frac{1}{2}$%, $1\frac{1}{4}$, 1.3, $\frac{11}{8}$
6. 42

Chapter 5

Pretest, page 32
1. $120
2. $45
3. $1,792.50
4. $525
5. $2,025
6. $1,665

Lesson 5.1, page 33
1. $16.50
2. $30.75
3. $8.36
4. $33.02
5. $68.40

Lesson 5.2, page 34
1. $665.50
2. $707.25
3. $463.98
4. $1,089.66
5. $1,413.60

Lesson 5.3, page 35
1. $385.31
2. $1,511.25
3. $2,658.50
4. $888.25
5. $816

Posttest, page 36
1. $275
2. $5,068.75
3. $6,200
4. $1,750
5. $1,375
6. $5,675

Mid-Test Chapters 1–5

Mid-Test, page 37
1. 1,555,700
2. 188,900
3. 2,733,600
4. 227,800
5. 11

6. 8

Mid-Test, page 38
1. 38
2. 6.8
3. 52
4. $\frac{112}{5}$
5. 57.12
6. 542

Mid-Test, page 39
1. $382.50
2. $438.75
3. $1,245
4. $2\frac{1}{2}$%
5. $1,580
6. $9,200

Mid-Test, page 40
1. 12
2. 12
3. 63
4. 27
5. 9
6. 30

Chapter 6

Pretest, page 41
1. 49
2. 22
3. 100
4. 12
5. 20
6. 6

Lesson 6.1, page 42
1. yes
2. no
3. yes
4. yes
5. 5

Lesson 6.2, page 43
1. 128
2. 24
3. 128
4. 12
5. 98

Lesson 6.3, page 44
1. 6
2. 4
3. 27
4. 126
5. 15

Grade 7 Answers

Posttest, page 45
1. 250
2. 140
3. 75
4. 6
5. 9
6. 36

Chapter 7

Pretest, page 46
1. 424
2. 7,392
3. 3.25
4. 11,700
5. 1.25
6. 5

Lesson 7.1, page 47
1. 27,984
2. 9,328
3. 540
4. 81
5. 4,464

Lesson 7.2, page 48
1. 8
2. 48
3. 12
4. 6
5. 12

Lesson 7.3, page 49
1. 2,260
2. 681.6
3. 0.079
4. 36,160
5. 19.2

Lesson 7.4, page 50
1. 138
2. 2.25
3. 2 days 15 hours
4. 324
5. 19,440

Posttest, page 51
1. 0.0368
2. 31,680
3. 1.25
4. 4,500
5. 0.75
6. 9

Chapter 8

Pretest, page 52
1. 0.0832
2. 7.05
3. 28,000
4. 0.028
5. 0.00055
6. 1,500

Lesson 8.1, page 53
1. 12,000
2. 45
3. 266,000
4. 0.38
5. 1,200,000

Lesson 8.2, page 54
1. 7
2. 10.5
3. 22,400
4. 0.055
5. 3,500

Lesson 8.3, page 55
1. 840
2. 42,000
3. 2,700
4. 0.011
5. 326,000

Posttest, page 56
1. 1,800
2. 2,100,000
3. 500
4. 500,000
5. 0.0164
6. 16,400

Chapter 9

Pretest, page 57
1. 12
2. Rock and Alternative
3. 6
4. 10
5. 36
6. 22

Pretest, page 58
1. $4\frac{1}{2}$
2. 2
3. $16\frac{1}{2}$
4. 6
5. 4
6. 4

Grade 7 Answers

Lesson 9.1, page 59
1. 100
2. 2
3. 8
4. 19
5. 9

Lesson 9.2, page 60
1. 6
2. 1
3. 19
4. 9
5. 3

Lesson 9.3, page 61
1. 7
2. 40
3. 1, 7, 9
4. 4
5. 3 and 4

Lesson 9.4, page 62
1. cranberry, blackberry
2. 80
3. 400
4. 160 people

Lesson 9.5, page 63
1. 75
2. 65, 80, 85
3. 6
4. 6
5. positive

Lesson 9.6, page 64
1. 70° F
2. 16° F
3. 70° F
4. 71° F
5. range

Lesson 9.7, page 65
1. 49
2. 11
3. 3
4. 7
5. 28.5

Lesson 9.8, page 66
1. 2
2. 9
3. 9
4. 14
5. 21.4%

Lesson 9.9, page 67
1. 2
2. 4
3. 44
4. 4
5. 9

Lesson 9.10, page 68
1. 14
2. 20
3. 6
4. 50%
5. 6

Lesson 9.11, page 69
1.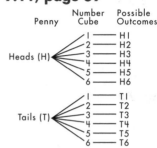
2. 12
3. 6
4. 8
5. 36

Lesson 9.12, page 70
1. $\frac{1}{4}$
2. 3:6
3. 0.125
4. 0%
5. 50%

Posttest, page 71
1. 7
2. 1 person
3. 11
4. 4
5. 3
6. 8

Posttest, page 72
1. 0.5
2. 1:3
3. $\frac{2}{3}$
4. $\frac{1}{6}$
5. 83.3%
6. 0.7

Chapter 10

Pretest, page 73
1. 60°
2. $\overrightarrow{ZY}$
3. acute
4. 70°
5. trapezoid
6. pentagon

Grade 7 Answers

Lesson 10.1, page 74
1. $\overrightarrow{AB}$ $\overrightarrow{BA}$
2. $\overline{G}$ $\overline{H}$
3. $\overline{JK}$, $\overline{KJ}$
4. $\overline{WX}$, $\overline{XW}$
5. $\overline{WX}$, $\overline{XW}$

Lesson 10.2, page 75
1. $\angle ABC$, $\angle CBA$
2. $\overrightarrow{MN}$
3. ⌐ $\angle ABC$
4. no
5. $\overrightarrow{LK}$, $\overrightarrow{LM}$

Lesson 10.3, page 76
1. acute angle
2. 25°
3. 140°, obtuse angle
4. 90°, right angle
5. acute

Lesson 10.4, page 77
1. $\angle DCA$ or $\angle ACD$
2. $\overrightarrow{OQ}$ and $\overrightarrow{OP}$
3. $\angle ACB$ or $\angle DCR$
4. supplementary
5. $\angle DCR$ or $\angle RCD$

Lesson 10.5, page 78
1. $\angle 6$
2. alternate exterior angles
3. $\angle 8$, $\angle 13$, $\angle 16$
4. $\angle 11$
5. $\overleftrightarrow{IJ}$ and $\overleftrightarrow{KL}$

Lesson 10.6, page 79
1. right
2. isosceles
3. scalene
4. obtuse scalene
5. All three sides will be congruent, and all three angles will be congruent.

Lesson 10.7, page 80
1.

   rhombus   square
2. Yes. A square is also a parallelogram with four right angles.
3. trapezoid, quadrilateral
4. quadrilateral, rectangle, parallelogram
5. Yes. A square is also a rhombus because a square has four congruent sides.

Lesson 10.8, page 81
1. decagon
2. nonagon
3.
4. pentagon
5. hexagon

Lesson 10.9, page 82
1. 3.3
2. The corresponding angles are not all congruent, and corresponding sides are not all proportional.
3. similar
4. not similar

Lesson 10.10, page 83
1. *I*
2. (4, 3)
3. *A*
4. *B*
5. (4, −2)

Lesson 10.11, page 84
1. reflection
2. translation
3. dilation
4. rotation
5. reflection

Posttest, page 85
1. right, isosceles triangle
2. not similar
3. rotation, (−1, −2)
4.

   D
       A
   B   C

Chapter 11

Pretest, page 86
1. 120
2. 81.64
3. 2,653.3
4. 104
5. 312
6. 152

Grade 7 Answers

Lesson 11.1, page 87
1. 340
2. 150
3. 130
4. 72
5. 150

Lesson 11.2, page 88
1. 35
2. 120
3. 432
4. 14
5. 25

Lesson 11.3, page 89
1. 540
2. 150
3. 6
4. 24
5. 126

Lesson 11.4, page 90
1. 125.6
2. 9.42
3. 25.12
4. 6
5. 50.24

Lesson 11.5, page 91
1. 78.5
2. 254.34
3. 12.56
4. 200.96
5. 452.16

Lesson 11.6, page 92
1. 1,200
2. 216
3. 80
4. 1,437.5
5. 10

Lesson 11.7, page 93
1. 3,056
2. 88
3. 488
4. 4
5. 142

Lesson 11.8, page 94
1. 120
2. 5
3. 270
4. 40
5. 20

Lesson 11.9, page 95
1. 800
2. 120
3. 105
4. 9.9
5. 40.5

Lesson 11.10, page 96
1. 13,345
2. 904.32
3. 3
4. 15.7
5. 1,186.92

Lesson 11.11, page 97
1. 2,009.6
2. 8,792
3. 480,812.5
4. 4
5. 942

Posttest, page 98
1. 24
2. 87.92
3. 63,360
4. 320
5. 21
6. 141.6; 100.8

Chapter 12

Pretest, page 99
1. $x - 5$
2. $y \div 4$
3. $n + 8 = 26$
4. $2(3) + 2(5) = 2(3 + 5)$
5. -8
6. $\frac{1}{4}$

Lesson 12.1, page 100
1. $c + 4$
2. $m - 5$
3. $72 - y = 45$
4. $d \div 3 = s$
5. $c > 2a$

Lesson 12.2, page 101
1. commutative property
2. multiplication property of zero
3. associative property
4. identity property
5. identity property

Lesson 12.3, page 102
1. $15(2 + 3)$
2. $a(4 + 7)$
3. $(5 \times 20) + (5 \times 2)$
4. $5(11 - 2)$
5. $8(v \times m) = (8 \times v) + (8 \times m)$

Grade 7 Answers

Lesson 12.4, page 103
1. 19
2. 8
3. 15
4. 14
5. 26

Lesson 12.5, page 104
1. 9
2. 20
3. 5
4. $3,650
5. 3

Lesson 12.6, page 105
1. 2
2. 6
3. 72
4. 6
5. 4

Lesson 12.7, page 106
1. 4
2. 25
3. −35
4. −4
5. 21

Lesson 12.8, page 107
1. 216
2. 256
3. 5^5
4. 2^6
5. $2^2 \times 2^3$

Lesson 12.9, page 108
1. $\frac{1}{2^3}$
2. $\frac{1}{8^2}$
3. $\frac{1}{125}$
4. $\frac{1}{729}$
5. $\frac{1}{36}$

Posttest, page 109
1. 10
2. $12 \div c$
3. 2^{11}
4. $48 - h = 32$
5. −3
6. 3^{-1} or $\frac{1}{3}$

Final Test Grade 7

Final Test, page 110
1. $17.16
2. 1.75
3. $2\frac{5}{6}$
4. $3\frac{9}{16}$

5. $2.33
6. 2.1

Final Test, page 111
1. 0.0042
2. 30%
3. 5,000
4. 580
5. 0.03
6. $575

Final Test, page 112
1. 7
2.

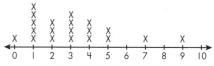

Hours of Exercise

3. 0.25; $\frac{1}{4}$
4. similar, dilation
5. 37.68; 113.04

Final Test, page 113
1. 86
2. 87
3.

Stems	Leaves
7	8 9
8	0 1 3 3 4 5 6 7 9
9	2 2 2 4 5 6

Key: 7|8 = 78

4. 18
5. 17%
6. 452.16; 703.36

Final Test, page 114
1. $\angle RST$ or $\angle TSR$
2. obtuse, scalene triangle
3. 5
4. 8
5. 5
6. 5

Final Test, page 115
1. 88; 384
2. 2($17 + $85)
3. $423
4. 13
5. 420
6. $\frac{1}{5}$